PRAISE FOR *THE BUY-IN ADVANTAGE*

"Most scaling companies fail because they can't get their people truly invested in the journey. Garrison's proven framework for creating genuine buy-in is exactly what leaders need to achieve sustainable growth."
–Verne Harnish, Founder, Entrepreneurs' Organization
(EO), and Author, *Scaling Up* (Rockefeller Habits 2.0)

"In my years leading successful high-growth teams, I've seen how lack of enthusiastic employee buy-in derails even the best thought-out strategies. *The Buy-In Advantage* offers concrete solutions to the engagement crisis holding most companies back."
–Joe Moglia, former CEO and Chairman, TD Ameritrade

"*The Buy-In Advantage* is a game-changer for any leader seeking to inspire a truly engaged team. Having worked to catalyze my own organization's culture, I've seen firsthand how a purposeful, collaborative approach can shift a team's mindset and elevate performance. Garrison's strategies for fostering a culture of shared purpose and clear communication mirror the core principles we embrace in our CEO culture, especially in aligning values and behaviors to drive excellence. This book is not just theory—it's a practical guide to cultivating a thriving, high-performance team. A must-read for anyone passionate about building a lasting culture of engagement and success."
–Jennifer Weng, President and CEO, Chief Executives Organization

"In my four decades leading organizations, I've seen how missed targets and turnover stem from lack of true buy-in. Garrison helps you solve the root causes standing in between you and what's possible for your organization. Highly recommended for any leader wanting to scale!"
–John Stanton, Founder and Chairman, Trilogy Partnerships,
and Chairman and Managing Partner, Seattle Mariners

"*The Buy-In Advantage* is the leadership guidebook I wish I'd had years ago. It offers a powerful framework leaders can use to consistently draw out the best ideas, solutions, and results from their employees. Highly recommended for any leader wanting game-changing results."

—Tom Leppert, Chairman, Austin Industries, and former
CEO, Turner Corporation and Kaplan, Inc.

"Having led a major company turnaround, I learned firsthand that culture drives results, and leaders drive culture. Garrison provides exactly what executives need: practical techniques to transform strategy into reality through genuine employee engagement. *The Buy-In Advantage* bridges the critical gap between having a great plan and actually executing it."

—Crystal Maggelet, CEO, Maverik and FJ Management

"Garrison's 'Collective Genius' process is exactly what companies need to find solutions to unlock their full potential. I've seen the impact and results firsthand in a dynamic board setting. A must-read for any leadership team serious about scaling."

—Tassos Economou, Global Chairman Emeritus,
Young Presidents Organization (YPO)

"*The Buy-In Advantage* is more than a book; it's a manual for leaders who understand that real change begins when people own the idea together. As a result of applying these techniques, our business is experiencing better outcomes, relationships, and results."

—Shari Levitin, Sales Strategist; Author, *Heart and Sell*; and
Guest Lecturer, Harvard Strategic Selling Course

"This book perfectly captures the current zeitgeist of widespread work dissatisfaction and its causes with both depth and breadth, providing concrete recommendations to leaders for building and bolstering the unity, cohesion, and trust in their teams. I highly recommend teams read this book together and channel the learnings toward specific improvements and growth."

—Erdin Beshimov, Founder, MIT Bootcamps, Massachusetts
Institute of Technology, and Founder, ClassHour

"Most leaders know that results are better when employees are engaged, but few know how to make this happen without grinding the organization to a halt. *The Buy-In Advantage* provides actionable ideas and tools that work"

THE BUY-IN ADVANTAGE

THE BUY-IN ADVANTAGE

Why Employees Stop Caring—and How Great Leaders Inspire Everyone to Give Their All

DAVE GARRISON

Matt Holt Books
An Imprint of BenBella Books, Inc.
Dallas, TX

Matt Holt is an imprint of BenBella Books, Inc.
8080 N. Central Expressway
Suite 1700
Dallas, TX 75206
benbellabooks.com
Send feedback to feedback@benbellabooks.com

BenBella and *Matt Holt* are federally registered trademarks.

Printed in the United States of America
10 9 8 7 6 5 4 3 2 1

Library of Congress Control Number: 2024055247
ISBN 978-1-63774-682-0 (hardcover)
ISBN 978-1-63774-683-7 (electronic)

Editing by Lydia Choi
Copyediting by Michael Fedison
Proofreading by Jenny Bridges and Denise Pangia
Text design and composition by Aaron Edmiston
Illustrations on pages 87 and 103 by Ralph Voltz
Cover design by Brigid Pearson
Printed by Lake Book Manufacturing

To Nancy, Emma, John Lee, Chanelle, Eleanor, and Team GG.
Thank you for encouraging me on this journey!

CONTENTS

INTRODUCTION

After two decades as a CEO of rapidly growing companies, followed by *another* decade of coaching, advising, and delivering workshops to thousands of leaders around the world, I've been on a lot of planes. In the *eight million* miles I've logged during that time, I've seen firsthand the problems faced by small- and medium-sized organizations. In fact, I've either experienced most imaginable problems myself as CEO, coached others through them, or discussed them as a board member for companies like Ameritrade. In many cases, all three.

Some of my clients run multibillion-dollar companies, many lead start-ups, and some lead departments or divisions within bigger companies. Some were born with a silver spoon, but most were not. Some have degrees from prestigious universities, but many never spent a day in college. Most have put in blood, sweat, and tears to lead organizations that are making a difference, whether in the manufacturing, services, retail, or nonprofit sectors. Regardless of industry or title, most face the same day-to-day challenges of juggling their "must do now" list with identifying and implementing new ideas that will hopefully drive long-term growth. And they all spend a *lot* of energy trying to figure out how to motivate their people and align everyone's priorities to make "great" happen.

Over the years I've heard the same concerns over and over from these clients: How do I get my people to stay focused on the most important stuff and not get bogged down with side issues? How do I get them to reach across silos and cooperate to accomplish our key priorities? How do we balance the need for short-term results while not losing track of initiatives that will drive significant improvements in the long run? How do we create time to grow people—and what does growing our people even look like?

Right after sharing such frustrations, they are usually quick to point out all the things that *are* working well. Here are some typical phrases they use to insist that they don't *really* have problems with their people . . .

I've hired a great team (though there may be one bad apple who needs replacing).
My people are happy.
We pay everyone fairly.
We are passionate about our customers.
We've invested in systems, software, and equipment.
We care about our people.
We always try to do the right thing.
We work really hard.

In reflecting on their wins and successes, it's easy for such leaders to dismiss their frustrations as fleeting and conclude that things were probably as good as they could ever get. I see the same pattern across companies of all stages, sizes, industries, and locations around the world. I've felt it myself. Working with thousands of leaders has proven to me the gap between potential and actual performance can be significantly narrowed. The concepts to achieve more of the raw potential of teams are not complicated, yet what's missing is the how.

But the solution would not be found in traditional motivational tactics such as offering higher bonuses, benefits like discounted lunches at work, or Friday afternoon beer blasts. Such tactics were appreciated, sure, but my clients found that they did not really move the needle on buy-in.

I experienced this personally during my 20 years as a CEO. Whenever I would have an idea to take the company to the next level, I would come in all excited and share it with those who would be responsible for making it happen. They would usually ask a few questions and give me a ho-hum, "Okay." A few weeks later I would check on the status of implementing the idea, only to find that it had ended up in the graveyard of other good ideas that got stuck and forgotten during implementation. In my frustration I'd sometimes resort to "PB&J management"—that is, the "patiently badger and jam it down their throats" method. This would get a more enthusiastic response of "We can do that." But yet again, when I'd follow up a few weeks later, I'd find little or no progress.

One day I was facilitating a forum retreat with a dozen executives who are members of the Young Presidents' Organization. I love these sessions because of the insightful conversations among bright, accomplished men and women. One talented entrepreneur summed up this universal problem of "ho-hum" better than I'd ever heard before: "Sometimes I feel like I'm leading my team up a mountain. But when I stop, turn around, and look downhill, they are mostly still at the foot of the mountain. Despite all my hard work and efforts to get them to follow me, they are way behind!"

THE SOLUTION: FOSTERING BUY-IN!

Looking back, I now realize that whenever my ideas to improve my company's results were not getting through, the big problem was lack of overall engagement and enthusiasm about our values and purpose. And without even knowing it, I was a contributor to this lack of engagement. Some call this the GAS (Give A Shit) Factor. Others refer to it as a lack of buy-in. Whatever you call it, it's what happens when an organization is not keeping up with the leader's passion and intensity. Some individuals or departments may have passion for their own parts of the business or the people they work with, but there's a clear lack of collective passion, clarity of direction, and intensity. It's not because they aren't good people or aren't experienced (they usually are!) but because they lack agreement on how to generate game-changing results.

This phenomenon can be especially frustrating for founders or owners who started their company from the ground up. Alignment of people around a common goal and shared passion used to be easy for most of them when the head count was less than 10 or 15 people. But things tend to get lost in translation as any organization grows. The CEO's carefully crafted strategy stops being fully understood or executed by the frontline people. New hires no longer care about or even understand the mission.

Departments become siloed and unsynchronized. And new ideas tend to come from the top down, instead of from frontline employees who might know processes and customer needs better than anyone else.

Fortunately, I learned within the first few years of my consulting practice that there are powerful techniques that could have addressed my frustrations as a CEO. This book is all about sharing those techniques and showing you how to get organization-wide commitment to implementing game-changing ideas.

I've honed the ideas in this book by spending a decade observing and working with an elite group of organizations that have overcome the confusion and malaise resulting from a of lack of buy-in, even while they scaled to great heights and large staffs. My firm has conducted extensive research and interviews to help identify what those buy-in-driven companies have in common. We've talked to their leaders and surveyed their teams to learn what sets them apart. Why do their people feel a passion that can't easily be extinguished by the forces of chaos that inevitably afflict organizations?

THE BUY-IN ADVANTAGE

We found out these organizations have succeeded in creating something we call the Buy-In Advantage. They have mastered tapping into the incredible potential of people and teams who are aligned, energized, and empowered! It gives them a leg up on the competition, better customer service, better financial results, and more freedom to pursue new ideas and innovation.

This book is the playbook I wish I'd had as a CEO. It describes how you can create the Buy-In Advantage for your organization—if you choose to. If I had had this playbook, the results would have been a culture with less stress, more effective work, and dramatically improved results. There would have been less wasted effort, more innovation, and less turnover. It would have freed up my time to work on those things I knew to be really important but that there never seemed to be enough time to get to.

Before you choose to commit to this journey, consider your leadership mindset for a moment. What do you really believe about the capabilities and potential of your people? Without the right mindset, the people on your team will see right through any new idea or trendy technique and pay lip service to it.

We believe an important part of any leader's job is to unleash human potential. This is accomplished by harnessing the collective experiences and insights of a team and applying them against a clear vision with smart objectives.

What does an organization with the Buy-In Advantage look like? From our experience in working with thousands of leaders, we've found three elements that indicate a culture firing on all cylinders:

1. Inspired people who focus on and achieve common goals
2. Leaders who focus on smart outcomes and criteria
3. Empowerment that delights customers and drives better results

Inspired People Who Focus on Common Goals

Every Cinco de Mayo, people celebrate Mexican traditions and culture. The day marks a significant and inspiring historical event—but it's not Mexico's independence day, as many assume. Instead, the fifth of May memorializes the day in 1862 when a poorly equipped Mexican army defeated a French army unit almost twice as large. The secret weapon of the Mexicans was the inspiration to defend their homeland.

Similarly, inspiration in organizations often comes from belief in a powerful purpose and commonly held values among team members. The focus on a common purpose and values provides clarity and predictability that reduces the amount of wasted effort. The opportunity for leaders, as we will discover, is to model including purpose and values into everyday conversation as decisions are made and priorities are set.

Leaders Who Focus on Smart Outcomes and Criteria

Great leaders know that their job is to show others the way and empower them to collaborate in getting there. Showing others the way is *not* the same as telling them, "This is the way we do things here." Instead, it's reminding them of the direction the organization is heading to achieve their purpose. It's also providing guardrails in evaluating alternative ways to get to that future state. These guardrails we call criteria—a concept we'll explore throughout the book.

Empowering others is like lighting up a charcoal fire on a summer grill. As each charcoal brick lights up, it ignites the others around it to contribute to the heat. In organizations, each person who reaches buy-in helps bring the next one toward buy-in as well.

Empowerment That Drives Both Impact and Morale

Inspired people allow an organization to improve its results, impact, and influence. Thus, there's an irony in any leader who tries to maintain strong control over everything that happens. By focusing on seizing and wielding power, such leaders actually decrease their own impact and influence. They extinguish the inspiration within their people, leading to an almost inevitable decrease in the output and results of the organization. Leaders who hunger for control and power limit the potential of their teams and what can be achieved.

Have you ever worked for a micromanager? You know, the clueless one who tells you exactly the way they want something done and then endlessly follows up: "Have you done it yet? Where do we stand on that thing I asked you about two weeks ago?" Micromanagers usually don't prioritize—every idea is of equal importance, so just get it all done! Another flavor of micromanager is the person who needs to approve everything. They will be heard saying things like "I didn't approve that" or "Who approved that?" Their need to weigh in on all decisions, though well intended, sends an unintentional message that everyone else is incompetent. This lack of faith in others requires them to make all the big and little decisions to "save" the organization.

I have worked for many types of micromanagers who wore me down. With each, I eventually reached the point where I gave up. I'd tell myself, "Just do what they say and call it good enough." I'd leave my best ideas and inspiration in the parking lot and lose all my enthusiasm at work. Those kinds of leaders are like a giant fire extinguisher on the sparks of inspiration.

We've all heard about legendary micromanagers such as Steve Jobs. Although micromanagers are notorious for their overcontrolling style, I'd argue that leaders like Jobs have a singular focus that they work relentlessly to execute in alignment with their compelling purpose. Jobs's *focus* was about clean design, simple capability, and affordable cost. When the iPod was being developed, engineers came back with a multi-button device that Jobs instantly shot down, insisting it have one control and an on/off switch. In other words, micromanaging is only helpful if it's laser focused and related to the compelling purpose. Otherwise, it can hold the company back and discourage innovation and engagement.

A big part of this book will be showing you how to tame any instincts you may have toward micromanagement so you can empower people and give them agency to excel. You'll see that the benefits include more time and capacity for leaders to focus on what's really important, both on and off the job.

We'll talk about the importance of having a clear, consistently reenforced, compelling purpose in chapter 10. Although a lot of organizations believe they have a purpose statement, it may surprise you that many leaders confuse compelling purpose and mission at the expense of their competitive advantage.

THE SHIFT FROM "IT'S TOO HARD" TO "IT'S A HABIT"

Let's start with the bad news: Change is hard. Changing habits is harder. Changing habits that involve other people is *even harder*.

The good news: change is only hard until it becomes a habit. That's what we tell our kids when they begin to ride a bicycle. It can seem overwhelming when they get on, try to balance and peddle, wobble frantically, and fall off. But if they stick with it for a while, the process gets easier. Soon they don't even have to think about how to ride a bike; it becomes an unconscious behavior. And the experience shifts from hard and stressful to fun.

There are some executives we meet who are *not* emotionally prepared to lead a buy-in-driven organization, just as some kids aren't yet emotionally prepared to ride a bike. Such bosses see their role as making decisions, solving problems, and controlling everything that goes on. And they don't want to hear any woo-woo crap about empowerment or purpose or winning the hearts and minds of their people. They think everything is working fine, and if anyone needs to change, it's their employees, not them.

If you are one of those people, you can stop reading here and pass this book along to someone else. But if you are willing to embrace change for the sake of building powerful new habits and far better results, get ready to enjoy the ride.

WHAT YOU WILL LEARN

This book offers three big promises that can give your organization a competitive advantage at very little cost by creating the Buy-In Advantage:

1. It reveals the major reasons why most companies fail to create and sustain buy-in.
2. It explains a systematic, proven solution to help leaders achieve buy-in, regardless of market conditions or industry-specific challenges.
3. It offers a practical road map for making this solution an entrenched part of a company's culture so the problems won't return in a month or a year.

We'll begin this journey in part 1 by exploring why so many companies struggle with buy-in, why a majority of employees don't really care about their work, and why a majority of companies are falling short of their full potential.

Then in part 2 you'll learn six powerful leadership techniques that will change the way you address common business challenges, with a new focus on boosting buy-in. These include inclusive brainstorming and decision-making, effective prioritizing to get more done with less distraction, rethinking your people processes to recruit better talent and retain them longer, and more. Even if you just begin by implementing two or three ideas from this section, including revisiting your company purpose, you will see a noticeable increase in buy-in and improved results.

Finally, part 3 will show you how to extend and sustain your buy-in culture through your everyday activities, even when things go off the rails (as they inevitably will, sooner or later).

PROGRESS BEGINS WITH A SINGLE STEP

Let's be realistic: *The Buy-In Advantage* won't benefit your company if all you do is read it. You will have to take active steps to apply what you'll be learning. But I'm *not* expecting you to apply everything all at once. That would be too time consuming and might even cause brain damage!

Instead, as a starting point, I urge you to gather your team together to analyze the current status of your business. What's working and what's not? What are the one or two chronic problems that, if addressed, would make the biggest impact? Gain alignment on those questions, then start gradually trying some of the practices described in parts 2 and 3. Simply having those group conversations and taking action to make a few things better will launch your people on an exciting path toward long-term improvement.

When applied with sincere effort, the strategies in this book will take pressure off a leadership team, create a more satisfying environment for employees, and foster greater and more consistent buy-in—all of which will drive sustainable bottom-line improvements for any kind of organization. You will enjoy a long-term competitive advantage that allows you to attract the best talent, retain them, get everyone pulling in the same direction, and even have an enjoyable time while working toward the same goals. (Yes, really!)

Part 1

THE CHRONIC PROBLEM OF LACK OF BUY-IN

Part 1 examines how we got to this current buy-in crisis and the substan-tial damage it's creating for both businesses and individuals. A fundamental need of business is to create the best possible results with the resources available, while a fundamental need of people is to have a sense of worth and value in how they invest their time and energy. When organizations lack buy-in, neither need is met.

The situation today is dire. The rate at which people change jobs or intend to change jobs has never been higher, and the rate of engagement as measured by Gallup is the lowest in a decade.[1] Additionally, the average annual rate of return for S&P 500 companies has averaged under 7% for decades![2]

With all the advances in technology, resources, training, and infra-structure, how did we get into this mess? On the surface, it may appear that there is nothing new here, as some of the reasons for our current buy-in crisis have been brewing for years. Yet the unique combination of events over the last decade and following the pandemic have created several new factors that most leaders may not be aware of.

In chapter 1, we examine the three factors that have come together to create a "perfect storm" and why a buy-in crisis now threatens to derail many organizations.

Chapter 2 considers how the usual approaches to combatting this cri-sis usually fail, including the four beliefs that create a chasm between lead-ers and employees.

Chapter 3 provides a diagnostic so you can evaluate how your organi-zation is weathering this storm and how much potential and bottom-line results might follow from addressing it and giving your team the Buy-In Advantage.

Chapter 1

THE PERFECT STORM NO ONE SAW COMING

On an ordinary morning in 2022, a leader for the Alta Equipment Group, which sells, rents, and repairs industrial and construction equipment from locations around the country (with more than 2,400 employees), found a typewritten letter among his usual piles of bills and junk mail. Written and signed by one of his 30 employees, it landed like a proverbial brick to the side of his head.

> *To Whom It May Concern,*
>
> *I am writing this letter to announce my departure from my position as Service Coordinator/Dispatcher. My last day of employment will be [date].*
>
> *I feel as if morale here is poor. I want to feel that I am in a positive, communicative, and supportive work environment and, after four months, I do not feel that here. I have been given additional duties that were not discussed upon hire, and ones that I could get paid more for, in a full-time position doing just that one duty, somewhere else.*

I feel that I have put in a lot of hours of hard work and my full effort is not appreciated, as management fails to give even the slightest praise to employees who do well. I feel as if every duty assigned is scrutinized down to the finest detail, and even when I try my hardest to ensure that the quality of work is excellent, there is still a flaw to be recognized.

I am a great worker and know my output is excellent, and I do not feel as if being put under a microscope for every single thing is fair to me or my co-workers. It feels as if management does not trust the employees.

I have seen many discrepancies in the way technicians are treated, and some of our technicians who are incapable of doing simple tasks are told "good job" while others who work, keep to themselves, and get their work done are told that they need to improve the way they're doing things. It seems that management does not realize the worth of its most valuable employees.

I will always be grateful for the opportunity to work here, and for the opportunity to be supported by such great coworkers who I now consider friends. I love dispatching and truly feel it is a career for me, but unfortunately, it cannot be here.

The letter was copied to her team leader, the regional vice president, which meant that the manager of this location (let's call him John) was going to be called on the carpet. It was also copied to their CEO, Ryan Greenawalt.

Years before, Ryan took a risk buying out the family business from his father and had methodically built the company by making a series of acquisitions and improving the service and economics at each one. He also takes pride in a carefully crafted culture that values mutual respect. The experience of this employee came nowhere close to his expectation.

During a subsequent call with his boss, the local manager, John, explained that the writer was a prized employee whom he had worked hard to recruit in a tight labor market. She was smart, detail-oriented, and driven to make things better—with the potential to become a future supervisor or location manager herself. He had no idea that she was unhappy. John prided himself on running a tight ship, as a no-nonsense, hard worker who had spent years serving his loyal customers in their New England town.

He considered himself a good manager. So he believed this disgruntled employee was an outlier, not a sign of any wider problem.

The regional VP knew he had to do more digging. Fortunately, the company's HR department had recently performed a survey of employee attitudes across all of their locations. The survey questions generated an overall morale score that could range from -100 (meaning everyone at that location was totally miserable) to +100 (meaning everyone was totally thrilled with their jobs). John's 30 employees had a morale score of -12, meaning that most would *not* recommend it as a place to work. And this rating didn't even include anyone who had quit before the survey! The location had a 30% annual turnover rate, which meant that hundreds of hours were being wasted on recruiting and training to fill all those openings caused by voluntary exits.

Things at the location might have appeared okay if you focused on its financial metrics rather than turnover. But clearly something was missing. Headquarters had invested in leadership development programs over the past several years, but John felt he didn't have time to pay attention to that stuff, given the ever-growing demands of real work on his plate every day. There would be time for leadership development when he finally got caught up. So John had stuck to the methods they had used for years, and everything seemed to be fine. At least until that letter arrived.

Fortunately, this story has a happy ending. Alta's senior executive team reached out to my firm for help and embraced real changes across the organization, with an emphasis on increasing and sustaining employee buy-in. Within a single year, turnover at John's location fell from 30% to under 10%, and their Net Engagement Score (a metric for how many employees would recommend the company as a place to work minus those who wouldn't) nearly tripled!

But what about all the other companies that never receive that kind of letter, because their unhappy employees leave without disclosing their true reasons?

"There are more lies told in the exit interview than anywhere else," a friend of mine reminded me one night at dinner, as we compared notes from our recent business experiences. Most often that lie sounds something like this: "Sorry, boss, I really like it here and appreciate what you've done for me, but I got a better offer for more money." Most people are naturally polite and would rather say they're leaving for more money (which no leader would take personally) than reveal that they started job hunting because of the way they were treated (which bosses take *very* personally).

This means that you can never assume your people are happy, even if they never tell you they're unhappy. You need to be vigilant for signs that the buy-in crisis has spread to your people.

WHAT'S CAUSING THE BUY-IN CRISIS?

At this point I want to stress that I don't lay the buy-in crisis at the feet of executives. Like the rest of us, most of them are doing the best they can to meet the demands put upon them. They lead people the way they were taught to lead in their youth, whether at business school or by emulating their own former bosses. But the workforce has now evolved, even if traditional leadership tactics haven't. Unfortunately, individual leaders are the most convenient scapegoat for broader trends that have been draining buy-in from most organizations over many years.

This buy-in crisis didn't happen all at once, like a flipped switch. It reminds me of how hurricanes start brewing off the coast of Africa as harmless low-pressure systems. With just the right conditions, like warm weather and steering winds, a perfect storm begins to form. But without those conditions it would remain just another cluster of thunderstorms. When you look at the forecasts for hurricanes and typhoons, all the computer models can give you is an educated guess about what might happen. But the actual path of a storm takes its own unpredictable course.

The conditions causing the buy-in crisis are not the result of just one thing. Don't believe anyone who blames the problem solely on the millennials and Generation Z, or the Covid pandemic, or the economy. They've all played a role, as did other, long-simmering trends, but it's the combination that has created a perfect storm. If we were to remove any of these elements, we would not be in crisis.

Generation Z is the fastest-growing part of the workforce, and they've been described as the first generation that doesn't put money first. Traditional bosses find them baffling, frustrating, and resistant to traditional management tactics. Gen Z doesn't see any stigma in changing jobs every year or two. And they don't see any point in being loyal.

The pandemic caused millions of people to start pondering big-picture questions they hadn't had time to consider before:

- *Is the time I spend commuting to the office worth what I find there?*
- *Is my company doing something I actually care about?*
- *Do the executives and my team leaders really care about my experiences and opinions?*

The economy has experienced wild gyrations in the last five years, from high unemployment to strong recovery to the worst inflation in four decades. The overall impact has been a widespread sense of uncertainty and insecurity. Almost no one really feels immune to mass layoffs caused by consumer shifts, new technologies, and/or foreign competition. Millions are anxious about their futures and have stopped believing that their employers are looking out for their best interests.

This abrupt shift in what work means to people, rapid changes in where work gets done, and the economic swings have never simultaneously occurred before. That's why we call it the perfect storm.

HOW LEADERS HAVE UNKNOWINGLY MISSED THE SIGNS

If the perfect storm for the workforce has been brewing for a while, how have even the most talented and capable leaders missed the signs? Well, many have been distracted by more urgent challenges that have occupied their focus. The supply shortages, the pandemic, global conflicts impacting supply chains, and worker shortages are just some of the short-term crises that led people to miss the longer-term trends.

I'd also argue that the origins of the crisis go much further back. For the last century, the business world has chased "big ideas" from thought leaders who promised new ways to solve every possible problem. Such ideas have included the quality movement, Six Sigma, reengineering, lean manufacturing, just-in-time inventory, AI, and many others. But none of those trendy ideas included focusing on the daily experience of employees—who are expected to do all the things that will delight customers and create profits.

Meanwhile, senior leaders have faced increasing pressure to drive short-term profits and shareholder value, rather than doing things that may not pay off for years to come. Most executive pay plans now include generous bonuses for exceeding targets such as net operating income, cash flow, or profit margin. And their performance is now tracked and evaluated more scientifically, using Management by Objectives (MBOs) or Objectives and Key Results (OKRs). The upside of this shift is that many leaders now have great clarity about what they are trying to accomplish and how they are doing. But the downside is that this pressure on short-term profits makes it an uphill battle to focus on changes in people and culture, whose impacts on the financial metrics (positive or negative) can take years to show up. It's easy to measure when labor costs have gone down 15% or sales have increased 12%, but much harder to track and reward changes in employee engagement and passion.

Along the way, what's gotten lost is the classic wisdom often attributed to Peter Drucker: "Culture eats strategy for breakfast." I take this to mean that whatever strategy is driving your MBOs or OKRs, you will *never* achieve the best possible outcomes if you don't take care of your people and culture.

By one estimate, the buy-in crisis is costing employers $450 billion a year—not even including the costs of turnover![1] I can't wrap my head around that number, so let's break it down. It equates to about $2,600 per employee per year in the United States alone. What would you rather spend that money on? And the measure of the damage is not only in money; it's also in workplace stress. Every time it takes weeks or months to fill an open position after someone quits, it means extra work for everyone else. And then it's extra work to train the new person and get them up to speed.

When employee needs are not recognized or addressed, we see workers turn to unions for support. Of course everyone has a right to unionize, but to me every desire to unionize is a failure of leadership. The only people who willingly pay dues to have someone else be their voice are people who feel like their voice is ignored or disrespected. People who fear for their jobs if they speak out. Unions are important in situations where leadership has failed to create a psychologically safe, healthy environment—but companies should be creating a lot more healthy environments even without the influence of unions.

This was true for entrepreneur Michael Hexner while building the retail tire chain Wheel Works. When faced with a union drive at one location, his attorney advised him, "You need to look more at fixing that than fighting the union." Michael didn't believe he had such an issue but, out of respect, he looked into that location more closely. "The manager was acting like a bully," Michael recounted. "We immediately stepped in and made changes and made the location a friendly place. When the union vote took place, we won with at least 80% of the employees voting for the shop to remain non-union."

Research shows that organizations that focus equally on objectives and healthy cultures are able to execute strategy more successfully and respond to change better than those that are numbers-only focused. A Grant Thornton study says the average large company could save over $100 million a year if employees were to describe their culture as healthy.[2] That should be enough to convince even the most old-school manager.

Yet what we sometimes observe is leaders clinging to "I have to tell them what to do because I have more experience" or, "My job is to solve problems" or, "I'll teach them by telling them." Even with good intent, none of these beliefs contribute to healthy cultures.

WHAT DOES BUY-IN REQUIRE?

Organizations have a good shot at beating the buy-in crisis if they can create three necessary conditions.

Condition One: Continual Growth Opportunities. Today's workers thirst for more variety and more mental stimulation. In the past six decades, the percentage of people with high school degrees has *doubled* to over 90% and the percentage with college degrees has *quadrupled* to over a third.[3] Yet with all this horsepower, most workplaces still break down jobs into simple repetitive tasks and don't really have a mechanism to tap into people's education. The workforce is not only better educated than ever, they are also better self-educated, thanks to the internet. This higher awareness leads to higher expectations about their workplace. People expect a variety of challenging opportunities, rather than just waiting to be told what to do. Yet leadership best practices have not caught up to this new reality.

Condition Two: Flexibility in Where Work Gets Done. These days people choose where to work based in part on flexibility in work location and schedule. If they need extra flexibility in order to provide for aging parents or school-age kids, they will choose jobs that make their lives easier. Employers still have the right to tell people where and when to work—but insisting on too much control results in an unintended cost of losing a large portion of your potential talent pool.

Conversely, providing employees with flexibility is a powerful competitive advantage in recruiting. Unemployment for college-educated workers has been trending down for a decade—it's a workers' market.[4] Employees are demanding flexibility, yet most employers are still trained to focus on other things. It's a massive disconnect that shows up in turnover, dissension, and dismal engagement rates.

Condition Three: Meaningful Work with Like-Minded People. More and more these days, work is about much more than getting a paycheck. Yes, competitive and fair pay is still a baseline for hiring, but it's no longer enough. There are two additional criteria now if you want to hire and retain people who seek meaning from their work. First, it's projecting a sense that the work means something and is worth doing. We see this in organizations where every person knows how the work benefits others. Meaning, purpose, and values matter more than ever. The second new criterion is creating a workplace where employees mostly like each other. This emotional need allows people to be themselves and give their all without a fear of being judged.

Together these three expectations by today's workforce have led to employer frustration, some of the lowest engagement rates in decades, and a climate in which employees jump ship the moment they find something that better fits their needs.

And when employers try to make things better, their efforts often backfire. Consider a Chicagoland pizza chain I know whose owner became deeply frustrated. The teens and twentysomethings she had hired to work as greeters and servers were attached to their phones. Instead of watching customers and anticipating their needs, these people had their eyes and ears glued to social media and text messages. When a customer would ask for something, it might take two or even three repetitions to get their intention. And even then, servers would often look at the floor and mumble instead of looking the customer in the eyes with a friendly response.

To try to get these frustrating employees to act like they gave a damn, the owner banned smartphones at work. This seemed like a fair request, given that they were making decent wages plus tips. From then on, everyone had to put their phone in a locker at the start of each shift and only check it during breaks.

But instead of solving this chronic lack of buy-in, the new policy made things even worse! Turnover went up sharply, as many jumped ship for similar jobs that would let them keep looking at their phones while working. And even those who didn't quit seemed more unhappy than ever, with their gloomy attitudes visible to every customer who interacted with them. Then sales started to drop, because who wants to eat in an environment full of unhappy people?

When the owner told me this unhappy story, she rolled her eyes. "I'm paying them to work—I shouldn't have to babysit them! They're ungrateful and immature!" Clearly, she had been taught that a leader's role was to tell people what to do, and she saw herself as a good boss. She organized the shifts, enforced the dress code, and established best practices for seating and serving customers. And if anyone didn't want to play by her rules, that was their problem, not hers.

Unfortunately, as leaders discover every day, it's actually everyone's problem.

WHAT IS LEADERSHIP, ANYWAY?

Before we go any further, allow me to share my definition of leadership. In my younger days I used to idolize Hollywood's version of military leaders, the kind who won World War II for the Allies. I pictured General Patton barking profanities along with his orders, and I figured that was a role model for civilian businesses.

Fortunately, I got a much more realistic sense of military leadership when I had the opportunity to work closely with the 4th Air Force Fighter Squadron at Hill Air Force Base in Utah. These amazing young men and women face the same handicaps as private sector businesses in getting around supply challenges, people issues, and bureaucratic red tape. They have to remain mission focused in the face of all kinds of distractions. And even high-ranking officers can't just bark orders and expect things to get done. The squadron's officers use informal leadership skills to win the engagement and enthusiasm of those several ranks below them. And the most respected people of all aren't even officers—they are the master sergeants who truly make things happen.

If these softer skills are essential in the military, with its strict hierarchy of ranks and chain of command, they are even more essential in business, where a title doesn't necessarily make anyone a leader. We've all met people whose title includes "Director" or "VP" or "Chief Something Officer" who we wouldn't trust to lead a three-car parade. Instead, my definition of leadership is the ability to provide direction, inspiration, and support to move people in a positive direction. Leaders at any level, with any job title, are able to work with others to maximize everyone's full potential toward a common goal.

Former general and president Dwight D. Eisenhower expressed it so well when he said, "The essence of leadership is to get others to do something because they think you want it done and because they know it is worthwhile doing."[5]

THE GOOD NEWS

The good news is that most of your competitors are making excuses on why they don't take action to fix their buy-in problems: their leaders tell each other that they don't have time to worry about culture, that now is not the right time, or that their people should just be grateful to have jobs.

Their ignorance or stubbornness creates an opportunity for you to use the proven methods to create your own Buy-In Advantage! It's an opportunity to have an unfair advantage in hiring, retention, and generating higher customer satisfaction. Pursuing buy-in will make your job as a leader so much easier when people are working with you instead of watching from the sidelines as spectators.

Creating this competitive advantage is ultimately what this book is all about.

In the next chapter, we'll look at how the traditional approach of trying to buy your way out of a buy-in crisis only works in the short term, if at all.

Ideas Worth Considering

1. As you reflect on your own business and career, what leadership trends have been most prominent? How has the quality of the employee experience been prioritized?

2. Consider your organization's policy on where work gets done. What impact has it had on your ability to recruit and retain the best talent? Does it need to apply to all team members all the time?

3. How has the better-educated workforce impacted the way you conduct business? What new challenges or opportunities are you experiencing?

Chapter 2

WHY LEADERS CAN'T BULLY OR BRIBE THEIR WAY OUT OF THIS

"Effective this Monday, we will strictly enforce the five days a week in-office policy."

While the good intent of this kind of announcement is to improve productivity by enabling people to collaborate, the unintended consequences are costly. Talented team members end up leaving the company in droves because of this dinosaur policy, for good reasons: the time and expense of commuting, the cost of childcare, and recognition their job did not require interaction with others in the office.

The cost to organizations putting this policy in place is not only unnecessary turnover and restricting their ability to choose from the best talent, but also lower profits. Research from Stanford University professor Nick Bloom suggests that hybrid work schedules increase productivity and create happier employees. He says the hybrid schedule to employees is like getting an 8% pay raise![1]

The "If you want to work here, you must be here all the time!" policy is a classic example of an organization trying to bully employees into showing more engagement, enthusiasm, and team spirit. Such tactics rarely work. Nor can trying to bribe people to feel more buy-in than they actually feel, such as via bonuses, prizes, or office perks like free food. Leaders who attempt such quick fixes don't understand what the data is telling us.

IT'S MOSTLY NOT ABOUT MONEY

I learned this surprising lesson early on in my consulting work. We were talking with a company that was growing and profitable but was vexed by a poor attitude and high turnover among its factory workers. The management team was talented and wanted to do their best.

The engagement survey we conducted found that workers strongly disagreed with the statement "I am paid fairly for my work." When we shared this data point with the leadership team, they were quite certain it explained all their problems. "We are competing for people with General Electric down the road. They pay much more and offer better benefits. The only way we can compete would be to spend a lot more on labor costs, which we can't afford." This is a common reaction: jumping to the conclusion that engagement problems are all about money.

But when we helped the company's leaders hold Discovery Sessions (a tactic we'll cover in chapter 6), we uncovered a lot more nuance about what their employees thought about their jobs. The leaders were shocked to learn that wages and benefits were a very minor source of their discontent. They were far more unhappy that the company didn't set each weekend's overtime schedule until Thursday, which gave them too little time to plan their personal lives around their overtime shifts. "What am I supposed to tell my son?" one worker asked. "I promised him I'd be at his ball game this weekend and just found out I have to work." Another complained about missing a long-scheduled family picnic. Single parents were frustrated about having to scramble for babysitters.

It turned out that the only reason for the short notice of overtime shifts was poor planning and forecasting, not any fundamental reason why they couldn't be scheduled (and, if necessary, traded) weeks in advance. This source of frustration and poor morale was fixable with very little effort and zero extra cost. Yet the leaders would have missed it had they just stuck to their assumption that people were disgruntled because GE workers made a little more. All it took to learn the truth was to ask—and truly listen.

At another company thousands of miles away, we saw the same kind of disconnect. Here the business-savvy human resources leader conducted a survey of all employees who had quit during the past year. The survey was just one simple question: *Why did you leave?* The top answer, not surprisingly, was to take another job that paid better. But a very close second was poor communication with their supervisor.

The HR leader was curious about these results, so he then surveyed the supervisors who had responsibility for all those who had left. When asked what the company might have done differently to retain those employees, the only response was higher pay. It was as if they couldn't even imagine nonfinancial reasons for quitting. They couldn't imagine that maybe all those people who said they were leaving for a better offer were lying to avoid an awkward conversation. They couldn't grasp the reality that most people today are looking for a sense of purpose in their work,[2] an environment where they have friends at work,[3] and the respect that comes from having their ideas heard.

That's what my daughter Emma, a millennial, experienced early in her career. When she informed her team leads that she had accepted a leadership role at another company whose values and actions were more aligned, they were surprised she was willing to leave for a significant pay cut. That decision not only gave her the opportunity for greater impact, but resulted in her eventually joining my own organization, so she could help other companies avoid these costly mistakes.

As we saw in the last chapter, very few people are brave enough to say, in essence, "Yes, my new job will give me a small pay raise, but I'm mostly leaving because I like the culture and people there better. My new team leader treats her people with respect and includes them in deciding how things should get done."

Data from the Gallup organization suggests that employees who feel buy-in require at least a 20% pay raise to be motivated to jump ship, while those who are unhappy require very little extra money to make a move.[4] So if it's not only about money, what is it about? It's about the experience of the workplace. As common sense might tell you, how people feel influences how much and how well people get stuff done. This means that leaders have far more influence over turnover rates than they usually assume, even if they have no budget to increase pay. It's good news that people rarely leave for money alone, because any organization can improve the more pressing reasons.

And yet shockingly few organizations understand this good news, because they lack the data to challenge their outdated assumptions about buy-in. So they continue to have a chronic disconnect between the leadership actions and employee reactions.

FOUR MYTHS THAT WIDEN THE CHASM BETWEEN LEADERS AND THEIR PEOPLE

We've seen four major reasons that contribute to this chasm between the typical employee's experience and the typical leader's beliefs about motivation and engagement. This chasm is usually *not* the result of leaders who don't care or don't work hard, or generational differences, or unrealistic expectations. Instead, the most common reasons are:

We are raised to believe authority figures have the answers. We are all taught to listen to and try to please our parents. We are taught to give teachers the right answer and get good grades. By the time we get to the workforce, it's natural to think that our main mission is to make the boss's life easier. That's how you get good performance reviews, and hopefully raises and promotions. As a result of this lifelong conditioning, employees often do their absolute best to do exactly what is asked of them from above. The cynical phrase about mid-level leadership is that they "kiss upward and kick downward." The idea of asking people below them about their experiences, and then incorporating their suggestions and needs into the game plan, rarely even occurs to most leaders.

We are taught to focus on traditional P&L statements. In many businesses, labor costs are among the top three costs, so of course they get lots of attention. The problem is that old-fashioned profit-and-loss accounting can bury the true causes that drive results. Those statements ignore the costs of high turnover, the additional burden placed on those who have to pick up the slack, and the wasted productivity of time spent training and retraining new hires. (Estimates vary widely but suggest that the cost of turnover can be as high as 1.5 times an employee's salary.)[5] As a result of this training, leaders spend a lot of time analyzing income statements, balance sheets, and similar metrics at the expense of studying data about their people.

We are told that the "war for talent" is all about money. "If we pay more, we'll get better people and keep them on staff longer" is a statement most business leaders would agree with. Yet, as we saw above, while employees do care about money, they care less than most leaders assume. Just as important, or close to it, is the culture they experience and the way they are treated from day to day. We don't always hear feedback about the pain of a talented team member who is missing the soccer game or the family picnic or who feels miserable every night because of a micromanaging or abusive boss. So the myth of money gets perpetuated and passed down, and those who lack buy-in have no incentive to share awkward or confrontational feedback. Once a money-driven culture is established, it can seem impossible to change from the perspective of frontline workers.

We are encouraged to ignore the people part of the productivity equation. Since the dawn of the industrial age, productivity has been measured by output divided by labor time, and the way to get more output in less time is by investing in new technology. Any machine that produces more widgets with fewer people is hailed as a huge boon for results. But leaders are rarely taught that improving organizational health can be just as big a game changer on productivity as any tech innovation. People who feel buy-in get better results in less time! This means that every bit of resources invested in employee engagement is just as valuable as investing in labor-saving equipment or process changes.

WHEN LEADERS ARE SKEPTICAL ABOUT THE "SOFT STUFF"

Sometimes I hear leaders say something like, "Yeah, I hear you—all this soft stuff might help. But we gotta focus on making money! That's the whole point of business, not making people feel warm and fuzzy!"

I was one of those leaders in my early years, so I get it. Based on my years of experience since then, I now offer two fact-based counterarguments. First, the current system of how most companies engage their people is directly responsible for their struggles to make as much money as they want to, or as they used to in better days. And, conversely, companies that proactively improve buy-in make more money. Gallup concluded that organizations with higher levels of engagement average a *23% higher profit than their peers.*[6] And, according to the groundbreaking book *Firms of Endearment*, companies that focus on people even outperform the stellar companies in Jim Collins's *Good to Great*—by sixfold![7]

So, even if you only care about money and don't *really* care about people, you should still be pursuing the Buy-In Advantage! And by the way, the return on invested capital—how much money businesses make based on what they invest—has averaged 6.6% since 1957![8] That doesn't sound like much given the risk and the amount of blood, sweat, and tears dedicated leaders put into their organizations. Maybe it's time to try something different.

I once had this discussion with a business owner at a Young Presidents' Organization gathering. He was deeply frustrated at his inability to reverse a damaging increase in employee turnover. After reading an article about the success of companies that provide employee amenities, he decided to invest in creating a more positive workplace. This wasn't easy for him, since he was very cost conscious and hated spending money on anything not directly related to the cost of producing his products. But he invested in adding a nice kitchen, a Ping-Pong table, and even a gym room that employees could use during breaks and after work. All that was on top of raising wages to match his competition.

The results? "After all of that increased spending, we still have a huge problem with turnover! I feel like people aren't grateful for what we've done for them." I asked if he had considered running a survey to find out how his employees really felt about their jobs, what mattered most to them, and why they thought turnover was too high. He had never even considered such a survey—which would have been far cheaper than his investments in new amenities.

Leaders who are skeptical of the "soft stuff" often think they can buy a better culture as easily as they might buy a new piece of labor-saving equipment. The data is clear: they can't. Even well-intentioned spending on pay and amenities won't fix a culture where people feel ignored, disrespected, left in the dark, or otherwise mistreated. People like perks, of course, but no well-stocked kitchen or Ping-Pong table can make someone feel good about a workplace that treats them badly.

CLOSING THE CHASM: WHAT EMPLOYEES REALLY WANT

So what's the alternative to trying to bully or bribe your way to increasing buy-in? Before we get to all the specific tools and processes you'll find later in the book, let's start with one simple principle and the three most common predictors of engaged employees.

Done With, Not Done To!

My favorite version of this principle is a quote about customer service by the internationally acclaimed restaurateur and consultant Will Guidara, author of *Unreasonable Hospitality*: "Our approach to service couldn't happen *to* them, it had to happen *for* them; we had to invite them, not force them."[9] This insight about customer service is equally true for employee engagement. No matter what wonderful things you want to do for others, people will feel more ownership if they co-create those experiences. *Employees want to feel like workplace changes are being done with them, not being done to them.*

More specifically, people want to be heard and included in decisions about how things are done. They want a leader who really cares about them. And they want opportunities to grow.

Being Heard and Included

After surveying thousands of employees across many industries over the past decade, my team found that a major predictor of an engaged employee is a supervisor who actually listens to their experiences. Specifically, when employees feel like their ideas are considered in how things get done, they are 50% more likely to be engaged and significantly more likely to remain with the company. Please note that this doesn't mean the person's ideas have to be adopted to make them feel more engaged! The simple act of seriously considering ideas that originate from the front lines conveys respect and boosts buy-in.

A Leader Who Really Cares

Another significant predictor of an engaged employee is an engaged supervisor. If a supervisor is simply going through the motions and doing what they're told, with no signs of engagement, that's impossible to hide from their team. As the representative of the entire organization, such a supervisor signals that it's perfectly fine to do the minimum required, not care about the outcome, and not make any suggestions for improvements. Our studies show that the engagement level of team members is typically about half of the supervisor's engagement level. This means that if you want an energized workforce, you need to make the engagement of your supervisors a top priority.

Opportunities to Grow

So what motivates team leaders? Once again, money is only one piece of the puzzle. Research from Nitin Nohria, former dean of Harvard Business School, suggests that indicators like being challenged, being recognized, opportunities for personal growth, and working with colleagues who will have their back are also important.[10]

We tested Nohria's theory with a group of executives in upstate New York who worked across a variety of industries. While the sample size was small, the results were striking. When asked to rank important factors in their work, money was not in the top six! Factors that were mentioned more often than money included:

- A stimulating job with challenging opportunities to learn and grow
- Collaborating with smart, personable people that I care about
- Transparency from leadership

We'll explore how to deliver all of those benefits in parts 2 and 3.

"But We Do Listen!"

Some leaders swear to us that they do listen to their employees. They'll explain that they have an open-door policy for anyone who wants to make a suggestion. Maybe they also have a dedicated email address for suggestions. Maybe they even have a quarterly or semi-annual town hall meeting, when people can ask senior management any question they want to.

Those are all fine ways to listen, but by themselves they won't create an environment that signals that employee input is highly valued. Open-door policies, suggestion email accounts, and town hall Q&A sessions all put the burden on individual employees to step up and stand out from the crowd, which few will feel comfortable doing. Likewise, running an employee survey but not sharing the results to the full staff implies that there was something to hide in the results. And doing a survey without taking any action on it is worse than not bothering with a survey at all.

For instance, one company with engagement scores well below the national average asked its branch leaders to meet with teams of employees to get their input on how to make things better. Great idea, right? But most of those branch leaders refused to prioritize that request because their performance was evaluated strictly on productivity. If employees started spending a lot of time in a supervisor's office to brainstorm suggestions, productivity would drop, and the leaders would appear to be underperforming their metrics. This short-term focus directly thwarted an opportunity for long-term improvement of results!

Awareness by leaders that they need to capture employee perspectives and suggestions is only part of the battle. You will also need a sincere, organization-wide *desire* to listen, which must be reflected in alignment of incentives and performance metrics at all levels. We'll show how to do that later in the book.

WHERE DO WE GO FROM HERE?

At this point you hopefully agree that the buy-in crisis is real, that it stems from many systematic sources and trends (aka the "perfect storm"), and that it's doing serious damage to countless companies, large and small, across every industry. You will also hopefully realize that you can't simply pressure your people to be more engaged at work or bribe their enthusiasm with quick fixes like increased pay or benefits that make the workplace more pleasant.

So what can you do to narrow the gap in enthusiasm between leaders and employees? The next key step is to find out just how bad the problem is at your specific organization. In the chapter that follows, you'll learn how to do the essential fact-finding and identify the eight most common warning signs of a dangerous lack of buy-in. The relatively small amount of time you invest will yield big insights from the experiences of your team that you otherwise may never discover.

Ideas Worth Considering

1. What do you already know from your exit interviews? Is there data to review about why people leave?
2. Does your organization currently measure the cost of turnover? If not, how would you calculate it, considering sourcing, interviewing, training, and lost productivity?
3. What ways do you encourage all leaders to focus on people as well as the metrics?

Chapter 3

HOW DO YOU KNOW IF YOU HAVE A PROBLEM?

Why is it so hard for leaders to know if they suffer from a buy-in problem? The big challenge is that buy-in metrics are not always obvious. Measuring profit, customer count, or number of employees is easy. Measuring buy-in is not. Some organizations rely on exit interviews to glean clues about engagement, which is better than nothing. But as we've seen, most people are polite and don't want to start a conflict with their employer—even on the way out the door. And if employees on the way out are likely to tell white lies about their experiences, that's vastly more true for those who stay.

There's an old leadership adage that every conflict has three perspectives: yours, mine, and the "real" truth. We usually get in trouble when we believe we can understand the other person's truth without asking them. Actually asking them about their perception teaches us a different way to see the same situation and can give us insight into where we may have blind spots. The downside is that it can feel discouraging—especially when we see things very differently. You will need to brace yourself to accept those new perspectives because, without them, you will be flying blind.

This chapter will not only help you know for sure if you have a buy-in problem, it will also help you understand the specific ways it's playing out in your organization.

At this point, you might be thinking, *This seems like too much work! I just need people to get s--- done and don't have time to understand their point of view! I've already got enough to do!* Here's my promise: in less than a week, you can gather all the information you need to determine if you have an opportunity to increase buy-in. If you already have an organization with high buy-in, congratulations! If not, the time you invest in making small improvements will pay off in improved results and less stress! More people will be working to achieve your highest-priority goals, and you'll feel less like you have to carry the load alone.

This chapter is divided into three steps that will help you understand your team's level of buy-in, whether that team includes five or five thousand people. First, you'll find a quick diagnostic that you can do on your own, consisting of eight common warning signs of a buy-in problem. We ask you to score yourself on those symptoms. Second, you can gather input from your leadership team via a short questionnaire that analyzes the organization from their perspective. We encourage both you and your fellow execs to complete this assessment and compare answers. (If you lead a small team and have no fellow execs, you can do this assessment on your own.) Finally, you will collect robust data from your entire workforce, either by surveying everyone or a representative sample.

By following the steps in this chapter, you will know exactly where you stand in less than a week. And you'll know how to apply the data you've collected to the strategies and tactics in the rest of the book. You and your team will be in a position to not only diagnose your specific situation, but also to prioritize action steps and start making immediate progress.

STEP 1: RECOGNIZING THE EIGHT COMMON WARNING SIGNS

As we've noted, you can't assess buy-in simply by asking a straightforward question like, "Are you bought into our goals and values?" Even anonymously, few people will give you an honest and detailed answer. Instead, you can start by observing everyday experiences that are red flags for a systemic, chronic problem with buy-in. In our experience with clients, we've found that there are eight common warning signs that typically manifest in most organizations. Do a thoughtful reflection and consider if, and how, these are showing up in your organization:

#1: *Wages are increasing but key talent keeps leaving anyway.*
We saw in the previous chapter that it's a mistake to assume people are exclusively or even mostly motivated by money. If a valued team member says they will leave if they don't get paid more, that's probably not the full story. Research suggests that it takes a competing offer of about 31% higher pay for a bought-in employee to leave, but far less to entice an unhappy person to jump ship.[1] And very few people are likely to be recruited by your competitors with offers of a 31% raise, especially if you've been steadily increasing your pay to keep up with inflation and your local labor market.

So, if you keep increasing pay but people are still leaving, it's not a money issue, and you can't solve it by offering even more money. Thinking you can is a trap, because anyone who joins or stays with your team only for the money will soon enough leave for more money. Instead, you will need to learn how to provide work that matters, opportunities to use their experience, and a culture of people they like and trust.

#2: *Meetings often start late, get canceled at the last minute, or run overtime.*
How organizations use people's time is an important determinant of how effective they will be in executing strategy and creating strategic advantage. According to research by Steven Rogelberg, professor at UNC Charlotte, most people say they hate meetings that are poorly organized and managed.[2] When meetings start late, those who came punctually waste their precious time waiting for others who consider themselves too important or too busy to make the same effort, or who are simply too thoughtless and disrespectful to consider the impact on everyone else.

Ineffective meetings are often the result of misalignment on how to address problems, set priorities, and keep a team from going down rabbit holes. We'll see how to overcome each of these in future chapters.

#3: *Key objectives or measures are frequently missed.*
This symptom is an important indicator of several dimensions of organizational health. I've observed that a lack of buy-in about goals and measures almost guarantees a cycle of poor performance, and then those frequent misses contribute to further demoralization.

If your key metrics are frequently missed, consider these questions:

- Were the objectives and measures realistic?
- Were they set collectively, by a single leader, or by a small group at the top?
- Were they well-defined with no ambiguity?
- Was there a clear prioritization of goals, or just a laundry list of competing priorities?

#4: *People do exactly what they are asked, but no more.*
It's difficult to tap into every person's full potential to significantly improve results unless you can harness their ideas and energy, not merely their compliance. Organizations get stuck when they subconsciously teach people to leave their full passion and imagination in the parking lot every morning because the only thing that counts is doing exactly what's asked of them. Here's a simple question: How often does a team member come to you on their own initiative to share an idea for reaching a current goal more effectively, or pursuing an entirely new goal? Once a week? Month? Year? Decade?

#5: *Engagement scores are low or declining.*
If you were to administer an engagement survey, how would the results compare to the average? Across most industrialized countries, the net percentage of employees who really care about their jobs is about one-third. The US average is also in the mid-30s and has not changed much in years.[3] If you have high buy-in, your net engagement score might be 60% or higher. If it's around 35%, you're average and will have plenty of room for improvement. If it's below 30%, you have an urgent problem.

#6: *People aren't clear on how the organization is making a difference.*
Seek out a relatively new team member and ask, "If a friend asked you about our company and what we do here, what would you tell them?" If they describe literally what the company does but have no sense of its broader

purpose, you probably have a buy-in problem. There's nothing wrong with an accurate description of your activities ("We build mousetraps"), but you also want to convey a sense of *why* your company engages in these activities—the point of doing it ("We're creating healthy environments"). This explanation of "why bother?" is critical to buy-in.

#7 *People are unaware of or confused about who is responsible for what.*
For every project or initiative worth doing, there needs to be one person, and one person only, accountable for progress and results. Does every strategy, every metric, every action have one clear owner? You've heard of too many cooks in the kitchen—the same applies to getting things done in a healthy organization.

It's easy for everyone to assume that someone else is responsible for getting something done. When goals are complex, it's easy for one individual or department to blame another for lack of input that creates a bottleneck. If things get stuck and there isn't clear accountability, you can end up with finger-pointing and defensiveness rather than problem-solving. That's a recipe for reducing mutual trust and teamwork, and boosting unhealthy rivalries—both of which reduce buy-in.

#8 *Key customers are leaving or cutting back.*
Like employees, customers are far more likely to express displeasure with actions rather than words. When they spend less money with you, or stop using your company altogether, that's a very serious danger sign. You need to figure out what has changed to drive them away, whether it's changes in their own needs, competitors' pricing, alternative solutions, service or product quality, or a hundred other things. Organizations with high levels of buy-in detect and respond to such changes quickly because customer-facing employees are on the lookout for problems. But companies with low buy-in miss out on catching and fixing early warning signals. They may have no idea something is wrong until a customer is gone for good.

At this point, take a minute to do an honest self-assessment of these eight warning signs. Are any of them major or even minor issues in your organization? Even in the healthiest organizations, most leaders are grappling with at least two or more of these challenges. They are worth addressing because, if left unchecked, they can balloon into a full-blown crisis.

Give yourself a rating on each of the eight warning signs by asking if the symptom is happening (all of the time = 5, most of the time = 4, some of the time = 3, occasionally = 2, none of the time = 1):

1. Wages are increasing but key talent keeps leaving anyway.
2. Meetings often start late, get canceled at the last minute, or run overtime.
3. Key objectives or measures are frequently missed
4. People do exactly what they are asked, but no more.
5. Engagement scores are low or declining.
6. People aren't clear on how the organization is making a difference.
7. People are unaware of or confused about who is responsible for what.
8. Key customers are leaving or cutting back.

If your score is less than 15, congratulations. The ideas in the rest of this book will help you maintain your high-functioning culture!

If your score is 15–25, your organization has some problems. You will be able to drive better results with less effort and less stress by applying the techniques in parts 2 and 3.

If your score is above 25, you have a very serious problem and should make buy-in your top leadership priority—starting now!

STEP 2: ASSESSING THE PERSPECTIVE OF YOUR LEADERSHIP TEAM

(If you work for a startup with no leadership team, you can skip to the next step.)

We've developed another brief diagnostic for members of a leadership team to fill out. Ask them to do it in advance of a meeting to discuss their perspectives on employee buy-in. At that meeting, start by asking each leader to share their total scores. Are they reasonably close, indicating a consensus about the health of the culture (good or bad)? Or do your top leaders have vastly divergent opinions? Which issues do they each think are the highest and lowest priorities to be addressed? Then encourage an open, judgment-free discussion of what informed each person's answers to each question.

Here's the diagnostic, using the same 1 to 5 scale as the prior self-assessment (5 = all of the time, 4 = most of the time, 3 = some of the time, 2 = occasionally, 1 = almost never:

1. We meet weekly and follow a disciplined meeting rhythm.
2. We regularly use effective and efficient techniques to capture everyone's best thinking in meetings.
3. We utilize a set of weekly metrics to help us gauge and predict the health of the business.
4. We build on each other's thinking in conversations as opposed to trying to convince others of our point of view.
5. We establish the criteria by which a good result will be judged before brainstorming solutions.
6. We set specific, quarterly goals that clearly state the activity, the measure, and the purpose.
7. We are comfortable holding each other accountable.
8. We use appropriate media or technology in virtual and in-person meetings to capture different ideas.
9. The leadership team has a unified understanding of the vision that has been properly cascaded and is known by everyone in the company.
10. We refer to our agreed-to values in everyday conversation as we make decisions and provide feedback.
11. Our team has a high degree of trust, and we are okay being vulnerable with each other without fear of judgment.
12. Our leadership team agrees on the profile and characteristics of the person or people who are buying our product or service.
13. The next two layers of the organization, those closest to the work, often bring forth new and innovative ideas and suggestions.
14. As leaders, we reinforce our organization's purpose and how our department's efforts relate to that purpose.
15. We are conscious of groupthink and, when in violent agreement,

we ask ourselves, "What would the opposing point of view do for us?"

16. We prepare and distribute information at least a day before meetings to allow everyone to consider the data and key questions.

17. We use processes to make sure all opinions are heard before making decisions.

18. At the end of each meeting, we identify what worked and what didn't in order to continually improve our sessions.

19. We have identified the key functions of our business, what must be done within each one in order to achieve our goals, and we have identified one person to be accountable for (not necessarily doing!) the work.

20. We consistently accomplish at least 80% of the goals we set each quarter.

For each question where your team's overall average is less than 4, select one or two statements you could improve on the most. Then, create a plan to address them. (Part 2 provides practical tools and solutions to help you with that plan.)

When you are successful changing your environment around those two statements, tackle two more!

STEP #3: THE BUY-IN ASSESSMENT FROM THE FRONT LINES

Sometimes it is difficult to see the issues that your team experiences. We often hear a leader predict that people in the organization are well aligned, only to find the opposite. That's why this step is so crucial, even if you've already gotten valuable insights from the previous two. This step will show you the employee experience from the employee perspective, which will be very useful as you build your road map of improvements.

If you're feeling some resistance to asking everyone these sensitive questions, I get it. I've been in your shoes and have felt the same resistance, as have many of our clients. But consider this: If you're in a new city and looking for a place to get dinner, would you rather trust the pitch on a restaurant's website or the collective ratings of hundreds of previous diners? Any individual customer might be biased or unreliable, but when you look at the sum total, you can feel much better about a restaurant with 4.7 stars versus one with 2.6 stars.

You will get similarly useful aggregate data by surveying all of your people about how they are experiencing the organization, how aligned they feel their team members and departments are, how purpose and values show up in the organization, whether their ideas and suggestions for improvement are heard and respected, and whether they'd recommend your organization as a place to work. Don't think of the results of this survey as carved in stone, but as an indicator of which areas you will need to prioritize for improvement. And don't be surprised if employee engagement is far lower than supervisor engagement; our firm's surveys consistently show that supervisors can have as much as twice the buy-in of the broader workforce. And it can be difficult for the executives to spot buy-in issues because their experience is so different from the perspective on the front lines.

We call this an "experience survey" to distinguish it from an engagement survey. It has only six questions and can easily be conducted online using SurveyMonkey or Google Forms, or even an old-fashioned paper form. Regardless of the survey method, this is a powerful option to get some quick feedback. If you have a small company, send the survey to everyone. If you have a couple hundred employees, send it at random to every third or fifth employee from an alphabetical list, depending on how many responses you are willing to read. That should be enough to give you a representative sample of employee opinion.

Beneath each question below is a guide to analyze the responses. If you are seeing a wide range of answers about your compelling purpose, values, or important priorities, you've got an opportunity to create far more alignment, clarity, and buy-in.

1. How would you describe why our work is important to someone you just met? What is our work all about?

Look for: *compelling purpose.* Do team members understand and feel a connection to the reason the work matters beyond money? If people can't tell you confidently why the work matters to them beyond their individual role, you have a serious (but fixable!) problem. We'll learn in later chapters why this is one of the keys to employee retention.

Please note that we define a compelling purpose as a clearly stated, succinct reason the work is important and has an impact on the world. Having one that everyone agrees upon is a clear hallmark of game-changing companies. Ideally, every employee—starting on their first day—will be able to explain why the work matters and what it means to them. And ideally no one will mention money as a compelling purpose.

2. How would you describe our company's values? What values do you experience in your day-to-day work?

Look for: *clarity of values.* Younger generations place a premium on working for organizations where they respect the values by which the firm operates. Ideally, your team members can easily summarize your values and give examples of how they show up in day-to-day activities. Even if they are only able to identify how one value shows up, count your organization as lucky compared to the average company.

Please note that we don't define values as the kinds of clichés that sometimes get printed on wall posters or pocket-sized cards. If your people need a poster or card to remember that you care about honesty, integrity, kindness, and so on, that's a sign that those values aren't really embedded in your daily practices. In game-changing organizations, values are simple, relatable, easily remembered, and universally known! We've found that alignment with an organization's values turns out to be very important to the buy-in levels of current and future employees. Consistency in how people treat each other increases confidence in the future and psychological safety.

The next four questions are asked on a scale of 1 to 10 where 10 = strongly agree and 1 = strongly disagree.

3. The people on my team agree on the most important priorities we are working on right now.

Look for: *departmental or team alignment.* We all like to feel a sense of alignment with our colleagues, whether as part of a work team, sports team, or any other kind of collective. If your people feel disconnected rather than aligned with their peers, that's a major indicator that they probably lack buy-in.

4. My opinion counts in how we get things done around here.

Look for: *a sense of being heard and seen.* This question will gauge if people

feel like they will be heard and treated respectfully if they make suggestions. Healthy organizations practice soliciting, sharing, and seriously considering diverse viewpoints before making decisions. Our research shows
that feeling heard is highly correlated to recommending the organization
as a great place to work.

**5. *My supervisor and I discuss new things I can learn each quarter and
where I can find opportunities for growth.***
Look for: *attention to personal priorities.* This is an indicator of whether the
organization has provided enough training and support to supervisors to
work with each individual on their personal development, for their own
good as well as the company's benefit. Please note that this is not about a
"performance improvement plan"—which is legal speak for "You're probably about to get fired, and we're creating a paper trail to prevent a lawsuit."
Personal priorities are usually about learning new skills, cross-training for
a new role, or advanced learning for eventual promotion.

6. *I would recommend this organization as a great place to work.*
Look for: *an overall positive work experience.* This question indicates how
confident people are in inviting others to share their work experience. Just
as you wouldn't recommend a restaurant to a friend after you had a bad
experience—even if you told the waiter or the owner that everything was
fine—neither would you recommend an unfulfilling or frustrating place to
work to a friend, or even to a stranger.

These six simple questions will give you a great launching pad for deeper
discussions about the employee experience and where you might begin to
replace any buy-in problems with the Buy-In Advantage.

GOING DEEPER: THE "LEARN BY LISTENING" TOUR

After you get the results of the Employee Experience Survey, you have the
option to go even deeper to gather more nuanced information, via what I
call a "learn by listening" tour. Visit some of the survey respondents, either
in person or virtually, and ask them to say more about their responses.
When you do, pay attention to their tone and body language. You might

also hear stories and examples of the kind of problems hinted at in the surveys.

Of course, if you have a low-trust workplace where people will be highly suspicious of a visit by the senior execs, this method is not likely to yield meaningful information. But if you start by explaining that your intent is not to get anyone in trouble, merely to better understand what it's really like to work at the company, you may be surprised at how much people open up. They just need to be convinced that you are really trying to make things better—from *their perspective*, not yours.

Do you see evidence that each department and team understands the company's overall strategy? Likewise, does each team member know how their work contributes to an important measure? You might meet people who like what they are doing, have a positive attitude, and do what they are asked. Yet at the same time, they may have no idea about the bigger picture they are expected to contribute toward, or which metrics will move the organization to accomplish its strategic objectives.

Do they feel comfortable engaging in proactive problem-solving, sharing their own new ideas, or taking advantage of a supervisor's open-door policy or an email suggestion box?

Ideally, several other senior execs can have similar discussions with other survey respondents, so you can have a wider range of conversations. After your listening tours are complete, meet as a team and share your notes. Did everyone hear similar responses? If not, how did the answers vary? Did any new points or examples raised in those conversations affect anyone's opinions about the scope and depth of your buy-in problem?

Perhaps most importantly, during those face-to-face chats, did people seem emotionally engaged or indifferent? Even if some or many of your employees seemed upset or angry about unpleasant workplace experiences, that's a far better sign than indifference or emotional detachment. If they still care enough to show anger or frustration or sadness, they will probably still care enough to embrace a turnaround plan.

WHAT TO DO WITH YOUR RESULTS

Congratulations on completing your self-assessment, your leadership team's assessment, your employee experience survey, and perhaps also a listening tour. You're already way ahead of the typical company in terms of being proactive about building a buy-in culture. Now take a few quiet minutes and make your own notes on the following questions:

- What were the greatest surprises?
- What data reinforced what you already believed or suspected?
- How aligned was the feedback across the three assessments?
- What are your biggest opportunities to address problems?
- What do you want to make sure to continue doing, or even double down on?

Remember, the *least* impactful way forward would be to have a group of well-meaning leaders come up with unilateral solutions in response to this research. It's far better to engage your wider teams in creating solutions. We'll turn to low-cost (or no-cost), proven methods you can put to work right away in parts 2 and 3.

Ideas Worth Considering

1. Did your leaders all have similar answers on the executive assessment? If there were dramatic differences between how each executive answered each question, why do you think they experience things differently?
2. What are the biggest areas of concern you can see from the responses of frontline employees? Are you willing to work on those areas first?
3. Where are your strong in buy-in indicators? What are you already doing that is driving this strength, and how can you reinforce those behaviors?
4. As we consider this data, how far apart are your executives and your frontline people in identifying the most urgent symptoms or problems to be addressed?

Part 2

BUILDING A BUY-IN CULTURE

Part 2 is about turning things around by working through the seven essential steps that build a culture of strong buy-in. These include several innovative tools pioneered by Garrison Growth, including the Drama-Free Problem-Solving System and the Discovery Session, a structured listening process that unlocks the best ideas of any team.

These and other tools enable leaders to leave behind the role of chief problem-solver, as their teams feel increasingly empowered to step up, speak up, and take initiative to make things better. Before long, the employee mindset shifts from "Just tell me what to do!" to "Let's figure out what's possible when we all pull in the same direction!" And unlike some of the outdated approaches we saw in chapter 2, these generally cost little or nothing, other than effort.

Chapter 4 begins by showing how to harness the incredible power of

Collective Genius. No matter how smart you are, I guarantee that you aren't as smart as everyone in your organization putting their heads together.

Chapter 5 shows how much time is wasted in organizations that endlessly debate ideas without reaching actionable conclusions that everyone can buy into. We offer a much faster and more effective solution—the Drama-Free Problem-Solving System—which works in any size department or organization.

Chapter 6 provides a proven process for getting off the treadmill of nonstop problem-solving, while accelerating the development of your people. The simple switch to focusing on questions instead of answers leads to consistently better outcomes, while also reducing the depressing feeling of "I'm working every waking minute, but I still don't have enough time to get it all done!"

Chapter 7 presents a foolproof method for prioritizing the few initiatives that can have the biggest possible impact on the success of your organization, while setting aside others for the future.

Chapter 8 explores tools that leaders can apply to bring people along on their journey, so everyone can take the initiative to contribute rather than waiting to be told what to do. We call this slowing down to speed up.

Chapter 9 considers why so many meetings are frustrating, ineffective, and a waste of time. By following our process to handle meetings very differently, you can become a master of truly impactful conversations that generate honest opinions, fresh ideas, and smart decisions.

Finally, chapter 10 provides a fresh take on the power of a compelling purpose and how to define purpose and values in such a way that your people will actually remember them and take them seriously. They can become a powerful competitive weapon in recruiting and retaining key talent. They will also make it easier to set priorities and navigate tough decisions.

As you read through part 2, I suggest taking notes on the strategies and tactics that feel most relevant to the current situation your organization is facing. You can then begin to put some of these practices to work immediately, for game-changing results.

Chapter 4

HARNESS THE POWER OF COLLECTIVE GENIUS

I've sat in (and conducted) too many meetings where people are wondering about the purpose of the discussion, what is expected of them, and what a great outcome would look like. Here's a typical scenario: It's time for planning and the leader calls for ideas on what strategies should be included for the following quarter. The team meets and people offer up suggestions. They discuss those suggestions and select one or two to pursue.

This may seem like a perfectly fine process, except that time usually runs out before all ideas can be heard, and time is usually wasted discussing ideas that will go nowhere. The question of what is most urgent to be addressed is merely implied, not spelled out to reach team alignment. Every person in the room sees the situation at least somewhat differently and offers ideas to solve different perceived problems. And not everyone will feel comfortable bringing their unique experiences and ideas to bear on challenges or to brainstorm new opportunities.

What would it be like if you could save dozens or even hundreds of hours by skipping over discussion of ideas you are never going to implement and getting right to "the good stuff"? What if you could solve more problems in less time with significantly better results? Especially if doing so was free to implement and not that hard to learn?

The only downside: a strong ego and thick skin are often required to be the kind of leader who consistently taps into Collective Genius. Abraham Lincoln had both; he was willing to be both vulnerable and curious, surrounding himself with smart people who strongly disagreed with him on important issues. Not only did they disagree with him, they sometimes did so openly in group meetings. Lincoln had the skill to collect opposite points of view in order to sharpen his own thinking. He didn't have the need to prove he was right. Instead, he had the curiosity to probe people on their beliefs in order to learn. He did not let his ego whisper in his ear, *I've got this*, and ignore others who had equally valid opinions.

In this chapter, we'll examine the mindset of leaders who are able to get the very best from their teams and harness their Collective Genius. We'll explore three principles that will help you authentically invite different viewpoints and facilitate getting them on the table. Then we'll provide a step-by-step process for tapping into that Collective Genius![1]

Collective Genius: A Mindset and a Process

In this chapter I talk about Collective Genius in two ways.

You will learn about the "Collective Genius Process" that Garrison Growth developed to help leaders elicit the best ideas from their people. This four-step process, which we have successfully used with many groups larger than five people, gets all options on the table and speeds up decision-making.

In addition to that formal process, there's also the broader mindset of "Collective Genius." While our process can be used in many settings, there will be times when it's not practical for some reason. In those cases, you can still set an intention and communicate in ways that give people permission to share their best ideas. This includes being curious, creating a safe space, and asking people to brainstorm on their own before group discussions.

Whether you follow our exact process or simply apply the broader intent, you will end up with significantly better ideas, discussions, decisions—and outcomes.

WHAT GOOGLE KNOWS ABOUT FOSTERING COLLECTIVE GENIUS

Google is the most successful data-collection and analytics company in the world. Their wide-ranging businesses are fueled by data and curiosity, so it's no surprise that Google researchers got curious about what they could learn from high-performing teams versus low-performing ones. Theories abounded before they launched an extensive research study. Some were sure that teams with the most diversity would be more effective. Others thought it would be teams with the brainiest people. Yet others believed it would be the teams that worked hardest or devoted the longest hours to projects.

As it turns out, what they called Project Aristotle[2] showed that the single biggest predictor of team success was psychological safety. This is the belief that it's safe for me to express my ideas in any work setting, even if I have a fear of looking stupid or "less than." When people don't fear retribution for sharing ideas, only then is the environment conducive to getting all ideas on the table. The more ideas on the table, the more likely that great ideas will be adopted, and the better a team's output.

This conclusion lines up with other research about how the human brain perceives situations that inform whether people can feel trust. It turns out that when the brain releases oxytocin, the fear of trusting others—even strangers—goes down. The Center for Neuroeconomics Studies even found a significant correlation between the level of trust in an organization and financial results. As the *Harvard Business Review* noted: "Compared with people at low-trust companies, people at high-trust companies report: 74% less stress, 106% more energy at work, 50% higher productivity . . . . 76% more engagement . . . [and] 40% less burnout."[3] In other words, environments of high trust are where the best outcomes occur.

So how can leaders create such environments?

THE MINDSET OF COLLECTIVE GENIUS LEADERSHIP

It starts with your beliefs, which influence the language you use and the actions you take. There are three essential beliefs to learn from leaders who consistently create an environment that enables Collective Genius:

1. All of us are smarter than any of us.
2. Our natural impulse to judge ideas defeats genius.
3. We cannot see our own blind spots.

Let's look at each in turn.

All of Us Are Smarter Than Any of Us

Most of us are familiar with people assessment tools that allow leaders to better understand the different gifts and perspectives that their people bring to the table. These include (among others) DISC, Myers-Briggs, Six Types of Working Genius, and Predictive Index. All highlight our different wiring as individuals and prove that there's a huge advantage in learning from people who see the world differently. That conclusion is a core element of Collective Genius.

When using the DISC evaluation, for example, you will learn that there is a natural team balance when some members are faster paced and don't want to wait for perfect data, while others want to do as much research as possible before making any decision. Likewise, people who focus on data will ask different questions than those who focus on empathy and other people's responses. You'll get similar insights if you apply Patrick Lencioni's model of different team contributors, which he calls the Six Types of Working Genius.

What matters isn't the specific model you use but embracing the fundamental belief that everyone has something to contribute and that everyone is worth asking for suggestions if you want to find the best possible solutions. To put these differences to work in creating great solutions requires the leader to shift from decision-maker to facilitator, and from idea generator to collector of other people's ideas.

Our Natural Impulse to Judge Ideas Defeats Genius

The second bad habit that interferes with tapping Collective Genius is evaluating ideas the moment they are proposed before fully understanding them. This is the opposite of creating an environment where no judgment occurs, also known as a "safe space." People won't share ideas if they believe their peers or leaders will pounce on them with negative or judgmental feedback. In contrast, in a safe space all ideas are recorded and considered with equal respect, and no one faces negative consequences simply for sharing their experiences or viewpoints.

Have you ever been in a meeting and heard, "We already tried that" or "We could never do that"? That might be the fastest possible way to shut down brainstorming. Such an attitude among an organization's leaders is also extremely destructive to creating a culture of buy-in.

I was once in London with a group of global CEOs, working to solve a challenge facing the Young Presidents' Organization. The discussion leader was a smart executive with degrees from Oxford and Stanford. But whenever anyone else offered an idea, he would either explain why it was wrong or tell us he had a better alternative. If you've ever worked for someone like that, you either learned the art of sucking up or you checked out because your ideas would never count.

Where do these soul-crushing bosses come from? Sometimes well-respected, successful employees get promoted to a fancy new role, and their higher status warps their self-perception. It's as if they've been hypnotized to believe *Now that I'm the leader, I must have all the answers.* That feeling is usually a reflection of their insecurity and a lack of training on alternative ways to express their ideas.

If you want to build enough trust to draw out lots of good ideas from across the organization, you have to walk the walk on *not* making snap judgments. The hard part will be practicing how to respond when you hear an idea that you think is naive, unhelpful, or flat-out wrong. If you want to keep your team sharing their creativity and experiences, silence the voice in your head that will sometimes scream, *That's a terrible idea!* Instead, switch on your curiosity: "Interesting idea! How did you come up with that one?"

Asking such questions might lead to some great new ideas, or a more viable variation on the same idea. But jumping directly to judgment and criticism will shut off the possibility of fully understanding before you have enough information. And it usually shuts down the contributor as well.

A Judgmental Mindset Uses Words Like	A Curious Mindset Uses Words Like
That will never work!	Interesting idea. Could you tell me more?
We tried that before, and . . .	What alternatives did you consider?
Actually, I've got a better idea!	What would this idea do for us?
Let's do this instead . . .	What did you mean when you said . . . ?

The amazing Walt Disney created a powerful process to foster creativity. He set aside three meeting rooms and assigned a specific purpose to each. In the first room, dreaming was encouraged—no judgment allowed. The second room was where his team addressed the question "How would we implement this idea?" The third room was where analysis, judgment, and criticism were welcome. By dividing the process into three parts, Disney offered his team a safe space to create while having a system of checks and balances to make sure only great ideas survived.[4]

My friend, bestselling author and sales futurist Shari Levitin, put Disney's process to work and came to an important realization:

> I used to bring my EA into Room 1 conversations with me and my visionary COO. . . We got animated and dreamed. "If we tried X, then we could do Y—can you imagine? We could be the biggest (fill in the blank) in the world!" But I came to realize that my EA was an excellent Room 2 and 3 person. She would think, OMG, who do I need to email about this? How will we have enough time for the idea? She would start blocking calendar dates. In fact, she got so nervous, she shut down and eventually stopped participating. Eventually, she gave her notice. Had we known about the three rooms, we would have saved her expertise for Rooms 2 and 3—and saved a wonderful employee.[5]

Remember, as author Laurence Heller says, curiosity and judgment cannot coexist.[6] Expressing judgment is like putting earplugs in your ears to cut off all input, including the opportunity to learn something valuable. In contrast, an environment that encourages the free exchange of ideas goes a long way toward fostering buy-in. When people feel like they've been treated equally and had their ideas considered fairly, they're committed to executing ideas even if said ideas are not their own. We find that nearly everyone likes the Collective Genius Process once they try it.

We Cannot See Our Own Blind Spots

I'm sure you've heard of being "blindsided" when something happens that we didn't see coming. How can this occur when we see so much? It's because the human brain literally creates its own blind spots.

Our five senses take in billions of bits of information every day, like giant vacuum cleaners sucking in everything around us. The brain has to apply a mechanism to sort through all this information so we won't get overwhelmed and can feel safe. The way we sort through the information is by discarding whatever our subconscious doesn't think we need. For instance, when you drive, your eyes see all the other cars, their license plates, their makes and models and colors, and the number of occupants in each. But you won't retain 99% of that visual input. All you really *need* to know at any given moment is: *Do I need to do something different because of what this car is doing?* So that's what your brain focuses on.

Similarly, when you drive to the supermarket, you look for a place to park. You see all the occupied spaces and the cars in them. While you *see* the models and colors of all of those cars, if I asked you to list them an hour later, you would almost certainly draw a blank. Your brain saw no need to move that data from short-term to long-term memory.

Many of our core beliefs form during childhood, and we often don't remember forming them. They may be silently running in the background and influencing our interpretations of every speck of data our brains take in. These beliefs act as filters to discard most of the data our senses take in. So it's especially valuable if someone else retains important data that your own brain has automatically discarded. It's not that someone else's memory is necessarily better or worse, just that their own experiences and lessons nudge them to pay attention to different details.

When challenges arise at work, as on a highway or in a parking lot, we consult all the experiences in our long-term memory to inform what we think we should do next. We rely on our own experiences, which are unique to us and us alone. Thus, how we sort data is unique to each individual—we can each make sense of the same situation very differently.

Imagine you are a fighter jet pilot. You control a powerful plane loaded with the latest hardware for enemy detection and a variety of weapons for different scenarios. However, you have one weakness: you are not able to turn your head very much because of your bulky helmet and a restrictive canopy. That's where the expression "I've got your six" comes from. It means someone you trust will cover your back ("six o'clock") and call out things you cannot see because of your blind spots.

Translated to a work context, sometimes our blind spots are missing data, perspectives, or experiences. A high-trust work environment allows people to support each other by covering each other's blind spots without fear of criticism or retribution. There should be no shame in not seeing everything immediately, just as there's no shame when a fighter pilot can't see his own six.

The other notable comparison is that every fighter pilot is supported by a team of outstanding specialists on the ground. They deliver expertise about the weather, target identification, acceptable risks, weapons, enemy capabilities, and potential surprises. Without all that support, even the best fighter pilot would be all alone in the sky and in very serious danger. So you should be grateful for every expert who can help you make more informed decisions.

Three Mindset Principles of the Buy-In Advantage Leader

1. All of us are smarter than any of us.
2. Our natural impulse to judge ideas defeats genius.
3. We cannot see our own blind spots.

APPLYING THESE THREE BELIEFS TO DRIVE COLLECTIVE GENIUS

Hopefully you're now convinced that seeing other perspectives and working collectively is critical to making the best decisions, because we all see different things and interpret them differently. But that doesn't make it easy to open your mind to those other perspectives.

Active listening is an art. It requires me to quiet my mind and not think about how I'm going to respond, nor start judging others' ideas prematurely. Even after years of applying Collective Genius, I still need to remind myself that the judging can't start until the understanding is complete. When I get busy or stressed, I still have a hard time hearing others' points of view. I sometimes hear their words but not their meaning—because my brain swaps in my own interpretation of their words.

The only way I can appreciate someone else's meaning is to tell them what I think I heard and ask them to verify that I got it right. Listening carefully enough to tell someone what I heard them say requires me to use their words, not mine. My interpretation of what someone else says is about me, not about them.

If you race to judge what people are saying, you cut off your ability to be curious. If you say, "I know what you mean," or, "I hear you," it's another version of "I got this" and confirms you understand the meaning you just made of what someone says, which is not necessarily their meaning! So I suggest that you quickly tap into different perspectives by asking questions that draw out the other person's train of thought. Especially during one-on-one meetings, these types of questions can allow your genius to be fueled from the insights of others.

Because most organizations don't tap into Collective Genius, most people have never experienced it. So it requires an extra effort for leaders to teach their people a new method of idea generation. However, the rewards are worth that extra effort. When people learn how to share and discuss their ideas in respectful ways, it can feel like a shot of pure energy. This process boosts team members' self-esteem, creates better thinking, enhances their sense of teamwork, and generates the satisfaction of contributing to better outcomes. It's hard to imagine getting better payoff from a single change in daily business practice. So now let's dig deeper into how the process works.

UNPACKING THE COLLECTIVE GENIUS PROCESS

As we'll soon see in chapter 5 on Drama-Free Problem-Solving, an important step in productive discussions is framing the question or issue at hand so that everyone is addressing the same thing. Then, armed with alignment on the question, you can lead a four-step Collective Genius Process that allows creative genius to be generated and collated. The beauty of this process is that there is no time wasted debating ideas, *unless and until you are discussing the consensus's best idea offered up*! The four steps are:

- Work silently on your own answers.
- Share your thoughts in small group settings.
- Do a large group report out.
- Weigh the ox (vote!).

The Collective Genius Process

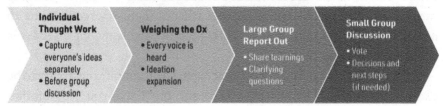

Individual Thought Work	Weighing the Ox	Large Group Report Out	Small Group Discussion
• Capture everyone's ideas separately • Before group discussion	• Every voice is heard • Ideation expansion	• Share learnings • Clarifying questions	• Vote • Decisions and next steps (if needed)

The first step is individual, private brainstorming. There is nothing worse than hearing a question and having someone shout out an answer before you've even had a chance to think about it. When this happens in a conversation, your brain turns to reacting to what others are saying. The better alternative is to take some quiet time to ponder and jot notes privately on the question at hand. Whether the time allocated for this step is five minutes, five days, or somewhere in between will depend on the specific situation. Regardless of the timing you agree to, what's critical is giving everyone on the team the opportunity to come up with their own ideas before anyone shares.

The second step (if the full team is larger than three or four people) is to break out into small groups to share your private perspectives. For example, if there are 18 people attending a meeting, try splitting up into three groups of four and two groups of three. Give each group time to trade each person's ideas among themselves and ask clarifying questions.

This intermediate step, between the individual and the full team, allows each contributor to hear and respond to questions that might sharpen or improve their thinking. These mini-groups might even find new insights by building on each other's ideas. The goal is to end this breakout session with no more than one or two suggestions per breakout group that every member can support.

The third step is to reconvene as a full team and have each mini-group list its best ideas on an easily seen location, like a whiteboard or flip chart. If you are in a virtual meeting, create a shareable document or slide that each mini-group can add to remotely. When all ideas have been posted, look for any that are so similar that they're almost identical, and merge them. *But you should still avoid any comments that pass judgment on the quality of these ideas.*

Finally, we call the fourth step "weighing the ox." The group leader should *still* forbid any discussion on the ideas that have been compiled because you don't want groupthink to influence how each member of the team evaluates each suggestion. Instead, give each participant three or four votes to apply to the ideas they find most appealing. Each person has the option to spread those votes around or concentrate them on a single idea that they feel very strongly about. Once you count up these votes, you will have an unbiased view of what the full group thinks of the suggestions compiled from everyone's individual expertise. Then you can finally delve into a full group discussion of the winning idea, including any potential problems and ways to make it even better.

What Does an Ox Have to Do with Identifying the Best Ideas?

Almost any group of reasonably intelligent people will have more collective insight than even an extremely smart individual. This widely seen phenomenon was the premise of James Surowiecki's influential book *The Wisdom of Crowds*. He describes a rural county fair in the north of England in the early 1900s. On display was a slaughtered ox, where a local statistician named Sir Francis Galton set up an experiment, asking passersby to guess the ox's weight. Not one of the hundreds of fairgoers who took a guess got close to the exact weight. But when Galton calculated the average of all the guesses, it was less than a single pound off from the ox's actual weight of 1,198 pounds.[7]

I tried a similar experiment in October 2020, a couple of weeks before the US presidential election. While facilitating a Zoom call with a couple dozen of my business school classmates, I asked everyone to guess who would win the popular vote and by how much. We had no discussion of the question before or after, and to my knowledge, no one on the call was a pollster. Everyone simply dropped their guesses into the Zoom chat, and they varied widely. But the average prediction was that Biden would win the popular vote by 4%—very close to his actual winning margin of 4.5%. That's Collective Genius.

This is why—as much as I value healthy discussion and debate—it's sometimes smarter *not* to discuss an entire list of proposed ideas. Sometimes it's better to poll participants without influencing them first and let the wisdom of crowds kick in. Your discussion time will then be better spent clarifying and refining whatever idea came out on top of the Collective Genius Process.

WHEN TO USE THE COLLECTIVE GENIUS PROCESS

This four-step process can be applied to generating values, purpose, departmental strategies, and any other important decisions. I've seen it help startups decide which product to develop next, and big companies decide which new country to enter next. I even used it with my own team to evaluate and improve the cover design for this book! In future chapters we'll return to this powerful tool in the context of other aspects of building a buy-in culture.[8]

For now, let me leave you with one more story.

Beau Johnson is a passionate leader who started his career working on construction sites as a tradesman. His natural talent for leadership was clearly visible to his coworkers, who encouraged him to become a union rep. Before long, more and more people recognized his talent; he was promoted to management and became a director. Beau's consistent thread in all these roles has been doing things right, putting quality first, and enforcing high standards.

When he needed some help to get his team to contribute more ideas, I introduced him to the Collective Genius Process. It felt pretty foreign to him at first. It ran against the mindset he had experienced from his first day on a construction site: the boss's job is to come up with ideas, and everyone else's job is to carry them out and make the boss happy. But to his credit, Beau was willing to try a new approach to leadership.

As he recalls:

> *From the beginning, I'm not gonna lie, I was skeptical. We had tried other methods before. This idea of Collective Genius didn't make me comfortable. But I learned that cultural change only sticks if it feels like everybody's idea, not just mine. For me, the big aha moment was when I realized that by trying to come up with all the ideas myself, I was really struggling. We were never gonna get to the next level that way. I had to stop focusing so much on myself and trust the process. The only true, genuine buy-in is when everybody comes up with a plan together.[9]*

Ideas Worth Considering

1. What do you already do (or what can you start doing) to encourage other points of view in making decisions?
2. Think of someone you know who is a great listener. What makes them a great listener? How do they make you feel like your ideas are really being heard and considered?
3. When someone brings you an idea, what words do you (or could you) use in response to better understand their experiences and perspectives?

Chapter 5

ADOPT A DRAMA-FREE PROBLEM-SOLVING SYSTEM

When I worked for a telecommunications company as a young executive, I was part of the weekly executive meetings held in a conference room decked out like we were at a Fortune 500 company (which we were not). We had plush chairs and coffee served in china. Despite the luxurious surroundings, those discussions were much like those at many other companies. The CEO had twenty years more experience than any of us and would come equipped with a list of issues he wanted to cover. Sometimes they were relevant news items; other times they were questions about performance.

If there was a performance problem, he might say something like, "We missed our revenue target by 5% last month. What are we going to do about it?" Then he would sit back with a Cheshire cat grin because he knew what was about to happen. It was as if we were the greyhounds and he had unleashed a mechanical rabbit we were all chasing. The "give the best answer and impress the execs" race was on!

The CEO was usually the first to share an opinion about the problem and how it should be solved. Others would then respond with a solicitous, "Great idea, boss, and you know what else we could do?" Usually, no one would ask for clarification about any idea previously offered but would merely pile on with more ideas. The executives were in enthusiastic selling mode as they each made the case for their own suggestions. And those not speaking would surreptitiously look at the CEO to see which ideas were resonating, as if the only thing that mattered was the competition to please the leader.

The sad thing for any company is that the silent folks in this kind of meeting are like spectators at a sporting event. Think of them as "sideliners." They certainly have ideas and insights based on their own unique experiences, but most are never heard by the full team. Personally, I was so disgusted by the groveling that I chose to be a sideliner. After each meeting, I would usually visit a colleague for a mini post-meeting. We would discuss what happened, comment on the public debate, and share different viewpoints, including our ideas about how to solve the "problem du jour" that were never brought up with the full group.

Looking back at those dynamics years later, I now realize that our inability to tap into *everyone's* expertise made our attempts at collective problem-solving doomed from the start. There was good intent behind asking the team for their ideas, but it never worked. There was a lack of mutual trust and no agreed-upon process for what it would take to achieve great decisions and solve timely issues. As in the majority of companies I know, everyone was locked into doing things the way they had always been done.

People often complain about well-intended yet poorly executed problem-solving attempts, dysfunctional meetings, and mediocre decisions—but they rarely try to adopt more effective approaches. This chapter explores a far better alternative: the Drama-Free Problem-Solving System.

"WHAT WILL A GREAT SOLUTION LOOK LIKE?"

Jeff Edison and his partner Mike Phillips had a dream to build a company that would buy, manage, and monetize shopping centers. Unlike competitors, they saw a niche in building a portfolio of shopping centers that were different from typical malls. Cincinnati-based Phillips Edison made grocery stores the anchor tenants of their centers, because no matter what happened in the economy, people would always have to eat. From that 1991 dream, Phillips Edison is currently one of the largest owners of grocery-anchored shopping centers in the United States.

Before the company went public several years ago, I was the strategic facilitator for their executive team's quarterly strategy session. Jeff kicked off the meeting by sharing some news with the group: "I wanted to let you know I've been thinking about adding someone new to our senior team. I'm interested in your thoughts."

The faces of the executive team all showed surprise and concern. I'm sure at least some were thinking, *Why do we need anyone else? Aren't we getting the job done?* I, too, was in suspense about Jeff's plan. I knew him to be a very thoughtful CEO who carefully considers all relevant options before making a decision. He was already much better at achieving buy-in than more typical senior leaders.

Before Jeff could share who he had in mind, I asked him, "Have you given this a lot of thought?" He had, so then I asked, "What kinds of criteria did you consider before choosing the person you think is the right one?" He shared three attributes for his ideal candidate to join the leadership team: credibility within the organization, a strong work ethic, and skills different from those of the current team members.

Next, I asked the team to reflect silently on one question: "If we were to add someone to the executive team, what criteria would we add to Jeff's list?" After a couple of minutes, we went around soliciting criteria, and I jotted the answers on the whiteboard. The list grew to seven criteria— Jeff's original three plus four new ones. The team then created a list of candidates who met all seven criteria. When we went around once more, the team named about ten internal candidates.

Jeff was delighted by how the team engaged in the process and produced a wider range of candidates using common criteria.

Let's unpack why this worked for Jeff and his team. Many leaders keep their brainstorming process to themselves and only share final decisions with their teams. Working for one of those leaders is tough. It's hard to offer alternatives or ask meaningful questions without understanding the considerations that have gone into the executive's new idea. When leaders keep their criteria hidden inside their own heads, the typical result is excessive, unnecessary debate, wasting everyone's time and raising their levels of stress and frustration.

But Jeff was looking for input *before* locking in a decision. Publicly collaborating on the criteria by which new ideas will be judged is a powerful source of buy-in. Highly effective teams discuss criteria first, asking each other: "What will a great solution look like?" They start with the *characteristics* of the solution before discussing actual potential solutions. This lays the groundwork so that everyone is solving the same problem. Without this key step, everyone may attempt to solve for their own preferred criteria, without expressing what those benchmarks are.

This discussion—tapping the full expertise of Jeff's team—is an example of the Drama-Free Problem-Solving System that Jeff and his senior leaders utilize, rather than flying solo and on autopilot. It also has the benefit of onboarding new team members more quickly, as they gain confidence about what's being solved before leaping into any conversations.

This system, which I've used during hundreds of client sessions, is pretty easy to implement. It only requires understanding five elements that result in gathering thoughtful ideas from everyone, leading to consistently better solutions:

1. Sharing critical information in advance
2. Leaving egos at the door
3. Avoiding sinkholes
4. Defining the key criteria
5. Killing snakes, not symptoms

Let's look at each in turn.

Element One: Sharing Critical Information in Advance

The first rule is that everyone should distribute key information about any significant problem at least a day before any discussion. Organizations that struggle with problem-solving often have people say in meetings, "Well, according to the data I've seen . . ." No one else can respond intelligently because they haven't seen that data! One person's exclusive knowledge becomes a weapon, or a tool of one-upmanship against everyone else. Private data hinders a drama-free exchange of ideas.

This can be explained by the way the human mind processes information. As the late Nobel Prize–winning psychologist Daniel Kahneman explained in his book *Thinking, Fast and Slow*, everyone's mind has two different ways to process incoming data. One type of processing is very fast—for instance, we can look out a window and conclude within milliseconds that it's raining. The same is true for memorized answers, such as to the questions "What's the capital of France?" or "What does 2 x 2 equal?" Those answers come quickly and easily, even while distracted by other activities.[1]

We are also capable of processing much more complex challenges, albeit in a slower fashion. The brain handles more complex, multidimensional questions that require multiple sources of information in a different way. If asked, "What does 1,182 x 729 equal?" you'll probably have to stop everything else you're doing and concentrate with a pencil and paper.

The reason this matters for drama-free problem-solving is that different, equally smart people process the same information in different ways. It helps to be mindful of different processing styles within any team, especially when it comes to complex, multifaceted problems.

Over the years, we've asked hundreds of leaders this question: "If I were to pass out a spreadsheet of data about your business, could you study it for just a minute and discuss it intelligently? Or would you rather sleep on it before discussing what it means?" Inevitably, between a third and a half say they only need a minute before discussing the data. The other half to two-thirds want to process it overnight. This means that if you surprise attendees at a meeting with new data, as many as two-thirds won't feel ready to offer their insights. The simple act of sharing data the day before will dramatically improve the quality of the discussion, if you value diverse contributions.

A second implication of Kahneman's work is that important decisions are best made using a process we call "second eyes." Even when people get key information in advance, some may need time to fully process the decisions made during a meeting. Therefore, it's valuable to add a standard process to relook at those decisions a couple of days later, rather than declaring all decisions to be final when the meeting concludes.

For instance, Underground Printing CEO Ryan Gregg would sometimes get frustrated when his executive team wasn't fully aligned, even after having some great discussions. They would thoroughly discuss a key issue and make a decision. Months later he'd hear, "Well, I never really agreed with it," or, "We should have done it differently." He wondered where they had gone wrong and where the comments were coming from. But the actual issue was that the discussion and decision took place at the same time. Those executives who process data overnight didn't have the opportunity to consider the full implications and unintended consequences of decisions. Once Underground Printing distributed information ahead and adopted a second eyes process for reviewing decisions, both the CEO and his executives reported much less internal dissonance and much more satisfaction with their problem-solving.

The positive impact of sharing complete information in advance and then using a "second eyes" process is hard to exaggerate. Team members who do their best thinking overnight will provide far better insights and will catch potential negative consequences before they can do any harm. So, whenever you have to wrestle with a significant problem, ask yourself three questions:

- What is the relevant information to share ahead of time?
- Who else on the team should be asked to share their critical information?
- Is there any analysis that can be done with the data before sharing it, such as highlighting trends, to assist the team during their preparation?

Then make sure that no decision in the meeting is final, and encourage everyone to submit second thoughts the next day.

Element Two: Leaving Egos at the Door

Ego is a major source of drama during attempts at collective problem-solving because subject-matter experts often get defensive about the correctness of their suggestions, and defensiveness tends to shut others down. This need to be right often becomes exaggerated in low-trust environments. The unintended consequence of this behavior is that junior staff or those in the minority feel shut down. They may feel uncomfortable challenging the supposedly expert opinions of people senior to them. This can cause an entire team to lose important perspectives.

Another common scenario: two outspoken team members begin to attack each other's ideas while aggressively promoting their own. When this happens, the rest of the team can feel like they're watching a tennis match, back and forth. Often one side may give up in frustration or exhaustion, but there's no real agreement or path forward.

Such problems are why former secretary of state Colin Powell liked to say, "Never let your ego get so close to your position that when your position goes, your ego goes with it."[2] But urging people to leave their egos at the door is easier said than done.

Imagine that you rush into a meeting in the middle of a busy day. If you're like me, you are in "list and attack" mode. I have a list in my head of what I need to get done, the conversations I need to have, issues I need to address. Attack mode is how I describe my desire to get shit done: boom, boom, boom. If I enter a meeting with this rapid-fire mindset, I unconsciously come across as a problem-solving machine. I am less aware of everyone around me and unintentionally cut off the benefits of others' solutions.

Here's a useful tactic for managing egos: ask the team to adopt a no-repeat rule. Anyone can bring up an idea once, but not over and over. That will cut the risk of tennis-style back-and-forth between people with competing positions.

High-performance teams get good at following General Powell's advice and disconnecting their egos from their potential solutions. Play down your own authority and signal that all ideas will be respectfully considered, regardless of where someone sits on the org chart.

Putting Buy-In Language to Work

A Judgmental Mindset Uses Words Like	A Curious Mindset Uses Words Like
What we have to do is . . .	One idea is . . .
We ought to . . .	What if we tried to . . .
I think we should . . .	We might consider . . .
What we did before that worked . . .	How is this situation different than when we . . .

Similarly, it's very helpful if the leader shares potential solutions last, after everyone else has had an opportunity to speak. My rule of thumb: leaders always go last, except when it comes to being vulnerable. When the leader offers their ideas first, even with all good intentions, it can suck everyone else's ideas and energy out of the room and redirect the conversation to merely clarifying and amplifying the leader's ideas.

This process takes a commitment to regular practice to be successful. Over time, trust will increase, which will increase your team's ability to deeply listen to and build on others' ideas.

Element Three: Avoiding Sinkholes

It's a challenge to solve a problem in a timely manner when the discussion goes off the agenda into tangents. You've been there: the biggest talkers dominate the room with whatever topic they decide to talk about. Then suddenly the discussion is over, and most attendees feel like they wasted their time on a wandering journey with no destination—despite the urgency of the issues that need solving.

Of course no one wants to waste time this way, even those who steer the discussion into these "sinkholes." But even if these tangents are unintentional, it's essential to avoid them during problem-solving sessions. Once you understand how teams tend to fall into sinkholes, it becomes a lot easier to sidestep them.

We work with a team that regularly runs out of time during problem-solving meetings. Usually one person will propose an idea, someone else comments on it, and then it turns into a free-for-all that eats up the rest of the meeting, at the expense of generating other ideas. This happens even when they follow the best practice of asking what the real issue is. At other times someone will come up with an off-the-wall idea sparked by the discussion, unrelated to the problem at hand. The team will then chase that tangent until the clock runs out.

One objective of the Drama-Free Problem-Solving System is to get as many ideas on the table as possible. If a team stops to discuss each idea in depth, it will be at the expense of identifying and drilling down into the highest potential idea, as selected by the Collective Genius Process we discussed in the last chapter. So we teach teams to capture each idea first, then rank them, and only then discuss the top one or two ideas.

Another common sinkhole is when someone has a great idea that happens to be off topic. I witnessed this with a client team that was trying to set objectives for the next quarter. We used the Collective Genius Process, and everyone brainstormed independently first, then in small groups, and finally by sharing with the full team. The result was two full pages of ideas for the quarter's top three or four priorities. Several were untested and somewhat radical but had the potential to be true game changers, such as reinventing its logistics process via artificial intelligence. Instead of pivoting the objectives of the meeting to discuss that provocative idea, however, we tabled it for a future meeting, so everyone could come prepared with essential data and devote the time that proposal deserved.

As we'll cover later on, a best practice is to put this type of idea on a separate list—sometimes called a "parking lot"—that collects any issue that deserves discussion, but not here and now. The key is to refer back to the parking lot frequently so people can feel confident that their ideas really will be revisited. This becomes easier if owners are assigned to each parking lot item that requires information to be prepared before it's discussed. The researcher can then schedule and invite people to a longer discussion.

Whenever you notice that a meeting is on the verge of falling into a sinkhole, politely interrupt the group with a question like, "May I ask a process question here? Is this an issue we should put into the parking lot?" You can also encourage the whole team to sound the alarm in those situations, perhaps by calling out a code word. If someone uses the code word to express their concern about a sinkhole, make sure you recognize and thank them publicly, even if you don't necessarily agree.

Best Practices for Using the Parking Lot Effectively

- If an idea comes up that is not on the agenda but has energy, put it in the parking lot.
- Capture the idea completely enough so that when you revisit it you will remember the details.

- Review the parking lot list before each recurring meeting to identify which issues might be important to include in the current agenda.
- Once every quarter, scrub the list and remove items no longer relevant.
- At the end of each meeting, ask, "Are any of these items ones that can be handled by one or two of us?" and, "Are any of these items to-dos that don't require discussion?"

Element Four: Defining the Key Criteria

Defining key criteria before you start to brainstorm is another simple yet powerful technique that can transform conversations and unlock better solutions. This was how we successfully redirected Jeff Edison's decision to add someone to his executive team.

Here's a situation I've been guilty of: I get really excited by an idea I learn about at a conference and share it with the team. It often falls flat because people don't catch on to its "brilliance," which frustrates me. In response, the team perceives my frustration and then shuts down. So the safest answer for those confused team members is simply to agree: "Yes, great idea!"

Everyone has criteria for solving a problem, even if those criteria are never consciously acknowledged or shared. Imagine a leader who puts out a call for solutions and quickly rips through a stack of ten proposals. Four are immediately set aside as "No way!" Three go into a "Perhaps, but they need some changes" pile. And the final three go into the "Really interesting! Let's pursue!" pile. Clearly, that leader is using an unspoken list of criteria, but to others, the results can seem arbitrary.

I've sat in hundreds of meetings where two intelligent, capable executives argue for the superiority of their points of view. And I realize that both are right, *depending on the criteria that define a good solution*. Without agreement on those criteria, they can go back and forth indefinitely without reaching consensus.

How much time would be saved if, instead of having your people guess what the boss is looking for, everyone knew the clear criteria that defined a great initiative or solution? You'd be far more likely to have people on the front lines take the initiative to propose operational improvements, potential new markets, or upgrades to existing products or services.

If you're trying to generate authentic, meaningful discussion about a new idea, you should first clearly identify what problem that idea is addressing. Next, draft a list of criteria for what a great solution to that problem would look like. Then share with the group both your definition of the problem and your current list of criteria. The team should be invited to build on the criteria list. Then and only then, ask the team to brainstorm their own solutions, in line with the agreed-upon criteria. While no one is likely to come up with your exact solution, this exercise is likely to generate more and better options than any one person could come up with on their own.

Criteria Considerations

The criteria we hear most often during problem-solving include:

- **Time:** How long will this solution take?
- **Difficulty:** What are our odds of successful implementation?
- **Resources:** Do we need additional help to get this done?
- **Budget:** Is there a limit on how much we can spend?
- **Unintended Consequences:** What could go wrong?
- **Purpose:** Does this get us closer to our overall goals?
- **Values:** Is this solution in alignment with our stated values?
- **Trade-offs:** What else *won't* get done if we pursue this?
- **Accountability:** Who will be responsible for us getting it done?

Co-creating criteria prior to any brainstorming will help clarify your thinking and enable your team to join in the process of creating viable solutions. And if someone proposes an idea that you hate, don't simply reject it out of hand. Get curious and ask about what criteria motivated that suggestion. Their answer may reveal additional criteria worth considering. Even if the idea doesn't fit, this process becomes a great way to develop decision-making and leadership skills.

Element Five: Killing Snakes, Not Symptoms

Jim Barksdale, the former CEO of Netscape, AT&T Wireless, and other companies, has a wonderful expression from his upbringing in rural Mississippi. When we worked together at Mobile Telecommunications Corporation, Jim used to say, "Dave, if you see a snake, you gotta kill it. That's rule number one. Rule number two is don't play with dead snakes."[3] He meant that it's tempting to focus on the symptoms of a problem rather than the underlying issue. But if we don't confront the underlying issue head-on, it will show up again and again. So drama-free problem-solving has to include identifying the actual snakes in any situation.

Most people in organizations can quickly identify the biggest snakes. Ask the team, "What are the issues that have been around a while that keep getting in our way of being great?"

For instance, the Garrison Growth team works with Aero-Graphics, an aerial mapping company that provides insights about the earth for urban planning, fire prevention, flood control, and many other important uses. One year, their executives gathered for an annual retreat and assessment of the prior business year. It was clear that sales to federal agencies were significantly below expectations. It was not a new problem. The team wanted to launch immediately into brainstorming solutions: let's hire more salespeople, raise the commission, target more agencies, run an ad campaign, and so on.

As their strategic facilitator, I asked them to pause and first consider the real issue that we were solving. The room broke off into small group huddles, then combined their insights to create a master list. The item that was voted most important to solve: "There is no plan for federal sales."

Had we found and killed the snake?

Not yet. We then asked for the root cause of why there was no plan. Again, we brainstormed, compared notes, and voted that the root cause of having no plan was that we had no agreement on what we meant when we said "plan." The issue didn't just show up in federal sales; it showed up in multiple places across the company!

It might not seem like it, but *plan* is an example of what I call a "trapdoor" word. Those are words that everyone understands, yet *everyone understands them differently*!

Checking for Trapdoor Words

Check your strategic plans, rocks, and objectives. Trapdoor words are those that are familiar to everyone and open to different interpretations. The challenge is that since everyone knows what they mean, rarely do we stop and ask, "What do you mean?"

Some trapdoor words: *communicate, implement, create, feedback, schedule, finalize, leverage, develop, strengthen, train, build, complete, analyze.* Do any of these appear in your strategic plans, rocks, and objectives without a clear explanation of:

- The evidence of the activity?
- What changes because it's completed?
- What measures we will see improve?

The only way to know for sure what someone means by one of those words is to ask clarifying questions.

So I asked the team to pause again and write down criteria for what a plan would look like. Was it a one-page outline, a PowerPoint presentation, a detailed ten-page road map, a spreadsheet budget, or something else? What details would it include? After a few minutes, we went around the room, and each person had a different definition of a plan. The team realized that the real underlying problem—the snake—was not the lack of a federal plan, but the lack of consensus on what the word *plan* really meant. This ambiguity could be seen in every other department of the business as well.

If the leadership had asked a team member to create a plan before they figured out what *plan* even meant, no one would have been fully satisfied with that plan—except its creator! While killing this snake of ambiguity was only the first step in solving the shortfall in federal sales, it was an essential first step. Once the Aero-Graphics team was aligned on the goal, they were able to move forward toward a workable solution.

Many highly effective teams go through a process of twice asking, "What's the real problem here?" to distinguish the snake from the symptoms. A useful clue: if similar symptoms are showing up in multiple parts of the organization at the same time, it's likely that none of those symptoms are the root cause. The Collective Genius Process is extremely helpful in these discussions.

There are several easy tactics to apply this insight to your own team. The next time you embark on problem-solving as a group, ask, "What's the real issue here?" and ask team members to generate their own lists. Then compare notes and list each idea publicly, without discussion. Ask the team to vote on which issue is most important to address. Then start an honest discussion: Is the root cause you've identified really the root cause? Or is there another snake that's even more fundamental?

PULLING IT ALL TOGETHER

As I said, none of these five elements are very complicated or hard to explain. Once you offer your people this path to drama-free problem-solving, most if not all should be willing to give them a try. And if anyone on your team isn't even willing to try, ask them what's getting in the way of testing this new approach. Maybe they enjoy drama a little too much!

Ideas Worth Considering

1. How well do we share key information in advance of meetings? Would a policy on the time frame for pre-reads help us? What kind of information should we share?
2. Where do we have opportunity to brainstorm criteria before solving problems? What's the best way to introduce this concept to our teams?
3. What issues are potential snakes that get in the way of our being great? (Hint: they are probably issues that everyone knows about, have been around a while, seem insurmountable, and show up in multiple parts of the business!)

Chapter 6

FOCUS ON QUESTIONS INSTEAD OF ANSWERS

For many years, on a typical Monday morning I used to go into my office armed with a long list of what I needed to get done. Like other Silicon Valley CEOs, the earlier I got there the better, because that meant fewer interruptions. As my team began to show up, people would inevitably pop into my office for a quick hello and to ask a question. I looked at them and tried to appear interested, but my mind was always stuck on whatever I was working on. Instead of having the patience to stop and really listen, I was paying half attention at best. When they'd get to their question, I'd automatically (almost zombie-like) draw on my experience and offer a solution that made sense to me, just to get them out the door quickly.

It was a short-term solution that ignored one of the most important lessons I would eventually learn about leadership: focus on asking questions instead of giving answers.

"Wait a sec," I sometimes hear from leaders when I deliver this advice. "I know more than the people who report to me. I have a lot more relevant experience, and I can save them time by cutting to the chase and telling them what to do. So why shouldn't I?" The simple answer is that a team that depends on you to make decisions and take action becomes an organizational liability. Giving answers is fine if your only goal is solving problems as quickly as possible. But as we've seen, that shouldn't be the only goal. It's just as important to generate buy-in, develop your people's ability to come up with answers, and to model tapping into multiple experiences. Plus, what you assume is the "best" answer might not really be the best answer because it does not consider important criteria you did not think about!

The dynamic of offering answers instead of asking questions plays out many times every day, in every kind of business. When rapid changes in customer demands, supply chains, or competitive challenges create disruptions, leaders are tempted to make snap decisions. Many were taught to "take the bull by the horns" rather than spend too much time discussing and debating. But those snap decisions can be highly counterproductive and lead to wasted resources and mistakes, while eroding rather than increasing buy-in among those who might have contributed better solutions.

In this chapter, we'll look at five scenarios where leaders can greatly benefit by focusing on questions instead of answers. The first two scenarios are "pop-ups" that happen spontaneously in the typical flow of day-to-day activity. The other three are structured, intentional opportunities that game-changing organizations can use to proactively generate buy-in, while also solving key problems. Let's consider them in turn:

- Using questions to neutralize recurring problems.
- Responding to proposed solutions without judgment.
- The "Instant Analysis" session: What's working? What's not?
- The "Seek to Understand" deep dive on a single challenge.
- A "Discovery Session" based on learnings from employee experiences.

EFFECTIVELY USING QUESTIONS TO SOLVE RECURRING PROBLEMS

A client I'll call Nick, the CFO of a medium-sized manufacturing company, was on the warpath when we started our coaching session on a summer afternoon. Just off a group call, he felt like it was the hundredth time he had heard the same excuses from the company's product managers. He told me that he had lost his temper: "We've talked about this problem for six quarters in a row! How can our inventory continue to climb? It's hurting our stock price! What about this situation don't you get?"

Although I had never been in his exact situation, I could easily identify with the frustration of conversations that felt like Groundhog Day—constantly repeating with no impact. Nick explained his exasperation: "I know I shouldn't have lost it, but these guys keep agreeing with my concern without solving the problem. Every quarter our inventory climbs again—it's really hurting our results."

It's always easier to see these dynamics at play as an outsider. Based on my experience, I asked Nick two questions:

Are the people in charge of inventory operating in the company's best interests as they understand them? His reply: "Yes, they're operating in the company's best interests as best they can. I know they're not hurting us intentionally."

As CFO, do you understand how, when, and why inventory is ordered? "Honestly, no. I'm not sure exactly how and when they place orders for inventory," he said. "I know there's a very long lead time, so there's always a risk of having too much or not enough. I think the product managers are under a lot of pressure from our VP of Sales to never run short. And they get better deals from manufacturers when they order more. The sales guys tend to make optimistic projections, so maybe that's why we always end up with too much."

After discussing the situation further, we realized that telling these managers that their results weren't good enough was, well, not good enough. Nick's complaints weren't changing their behavior. Their choices of what to do were perfectly consistent with their beliefs. Maybe the managers had subconsciously decided that the worst outcome would be getting yelled at by the sales department for under-ordering and messing up their customers. Maybe they saw a quarterly spanking from the CFO as merely an unpleasant inconvenience. It's discovering these beliefs and reframing them where real change could occur.

Nick added that of course he didn't want to hamper the sales effort or annoy their customers. There had to be a way to reduce excess inventory without those negative consequences, but he didn't know what it was. We reviewed the drama-free tools from the last chapter and used the opportunity to ask questions to solve the problem collectively, not unilaterally.

We agreed that Nick would set up another meeting with his managers, but with a very different approach. This time he would simply ask them to teach him what drove their day-to-day inventory ordering process. As they explained the details and nuances, Nick could ask questions to clarify the underlying beliefs that drove their decisions.

Sure enough, at that meeting, Nick learned that inventory management was only a relatively small part of the workload of the product managers. He also discovered that they had no formal process for deciding when inventory should be ordered. They were essentially winging it based on requests from the sales department. Armed with these insights, Nick asked them what additional resources or processes might help them make more accurate ordering decisions. They started to work out a viable plan for solving the inventory problem without damaging sales or customer service.

That's the power of assuming good intent and starting with questions instead of answers. Trying to get others to behave in ways that contradicted their beliefs was like trying to roll a giant rock up a hill. All it could lead to was their frustration and disengagement by all parties. The frustration was probably even an incentive for some to look for new jobs.

Asking questions backfires if you think you already know the answer and are trying to lead your people to your predetermined solution. This method of faking interest will quickly be seen as disingenuous. It will destroy trust, undermine buy-in, and leave the best answers unspoken.

On the other hand, asking questions about how people are actually doing their work allows you to better understand the obstacles that get in their way. Such questions encourage them to think about things differently and feel supported. It's like a two-way classroom where they get the benefit of your experience (in the form of your helpful questions), and you get the benefit of their hands-on knowledge.

The opportunity in working with Nick was to reframe the issue. He was able to change his mindset from one of judgment ("What are these guys thinking? Do we need to replace them?") to one of curiosity ("What's driving this behavior, if these are smart people trying their best?"). If you want lasting change rather than a short-term venting of your frustrations, you will have to recast your attitude, get curious, and ask more questions.

RESPONDING TO PROPOSED SOLUTIONS WITHOUT JUDGMENT

The second scenario we'll consider is when someone comes to see you with a problem. I often hear leaders say, "I tell my people that if they want to come to me with a problem, they should also come prepared with a solution." That's a great step—and one I was told to use as a CEO—but it doesn't go far enough to foster buy-in. The big question is how you respond when someone proposes a solution. Were you taught that leadership requires evaluating the offered solution and, if you find it lacking, counteroffering a better idea? If so, you are not alone. And, unfortunately, the shelf life of that advice has expired and will contribute to an erosion of buy-in.

One essential principle of leadership we referenced before is that *judgment and curiosity cannot coexist.* In other words, if you are already "sure" of what's going on in a situation, you have lost the ability to learn. Judgment leads to telling others what's what and what to do.

Of course, there will be times when giving your own opinion is absolutely the right thing to do. If the situation is truly urgent—like a toxic chemical leak—and you know what to do, give the right answer immediately! But most business problems aren't like toxic leaks. You have time to balance the problem at hand with the need to develop and grow your people, so the organization can benefit from a new generation of good leaders.

In addition to the leader-developing benefits of asking more questions in this scenario, you may also land on better solutions. Even if you have vastly more experience than your people, you don't have the *same* experience as they do. You don't know what they've done, seen, and learned. As we saw in chapter 4, this is an opportunity to tap into Collective Genius. Your own insights *might* lead you to the optimal outcome, but it's quite possible that someone else on your team has a better solution. You won't know unless you go through the process of asking smart questions first.

Leaders who commit to generating buy-in treat a spontaneous problem-solving discussion as a golden opportunity, in two ways. First, it's a chance to gain keen insight into someone else's thinking process.

Second, it's a teaching and learning moment for both of you. Solving prob-lems is valuable, but teaching other people to solve their own problems is even more valuable. And we know that adults learn best when they are self-taught rather than force-fed a solution by a more experienced expert.

Phrases to Use When You Hear What Sounds Like a "Bad Idea"

A Judgmental Mindset Uses Phrases Like	A Curious Mindset Uses Phrases Like
Don't you have any other ideas?	What other options did you consider?
What were you thinking?	What criteria did you use to narrow down options?
Why did you choose that one?	How did you select the option you did?
What could that possibly do for us?	What results do you expect when we implement it?

The answers will give you keen insight into how this person thinks about challenges. You will learn what kinds of additional discussion would be of most use to them. And you will also have a road map for the kind of discussion that will enable the other person to *challenge their own thinking*.

We are always teaching others how to interact with us, whether we are aware of it or not. If one or more solutions they bring up don't make sense to you, don't berate them for ignoring some criteria that you consider essential. That's teaching them that only perfected, curated ideas should be proposed and then only if they are certain. Instead, gently bring up the missing criteria for additional consideration. It might sound like this: "I agree with you that X and Y are important criteria for any solution. I won-der if we should also be considering Z. Do you think Z is significant as well? If so, how might that change the list of options you've generated?" If the other person prefers to process information overnight, ask them to take some time to consider the additional criteria, and schedule a follow-up session about how their thinking on possible solutions may have changed.

As leaders, whenever we're approached with a question or suggestion, we always have the opportunity to consider impact before responding. If we respond with a snap judgment, we're hurting our goals of fostering buy-in and deeper understanding.

You'll never guess
someone else's
EXPERIENCE.

And if you can't
UNDERSTAND
it, you'll be guessing at
necessary changes to
IMPROVE RESULTS.

That's like shooting at a target
while blindfolded.

The powerful result of asking more questions is that the leader teaches people to think for themselves. Even if—*especially if*—their proposed solution is not the one you would have come up with, try to approve it unless you foresee serious damage. By letting them run with their own idea, each of you will learn from the results. You might land on a much better outcome than the one you'd have gotten by imposing your snap judgment.

THE "INSTANT ANALYSIS" SESSION: WHAT'S WORKING? WHAT'S NOT?

Now let's shift from spontaneous, "pop-up" scenarios to more formal processes for stressing questions instead of answers, to elicit better solutions while fostering buy-in.

The first kind of feedback process is what I call the Instant Analysis session. This is when you ask each team member to prepare in advance a list of "what's working" and "what's not working" in the business right now—as if they were outside consultants. This means they are not analyzing the situation in their area but for the business overall. By "in the business" we mean both internal and external factors, which might include anything from products to communications practices to relations with a key supplier.

The leader goes around and asks each person to celebrate one thing that's working well right now, as well as flag one pain point that requires attention. This round robin continues until all ideas are on the board. (And when I say on the board, it's best the lists are visible to all and not on your notepad or a computer. This visibility will be important later.) The "what's working" list becomes an important reference of what needs to continue despite new challenges that come up. Once the "what's working" list is reviewed, the group turns to prioritizing the "what's not working" list. After the group has a chance to review and ask clarifying questions (no discussion, please, just clarification!) about what's not working, look for opportunities to combine like items.

The bright line test of what to combine is to ask the question: Could one be true without the other? If two items are similar but not the same, they should not be combined. With your newly combined list, take a vote of the biggest pain point—or the three biggest, if you have a big list to prioritize. We recommend having team members come up to the board and physically place their votes with hash marks in order to physically commit to their ideas.

You now have an action list of critical pain points that's been created and vetted by the people most affected by them, without any distortions that leaders might get from being too far removed from the day-to-day action. This list will be a valuable reference in prioritizing issues, planning strategy, and improving the business, as we will see in future chapters.

We recommend running this Instant Analysis process at least quarterly, but monthly is even better. It's a powerful tool within departments and even more powerful cross-departmentally as a way to establish cross-functional priorities and make midcourse corrections.

The Instant Analysis of "what's working, what's not" is a tool we will see later on in order to improve meetings—the biggest time waster in most organizations!

THE "SEEK TO UNDERSTAND" DEEP DIVE ON A SINGLE CHALLENGE

An Instant Analysis session asks a very general question: What is and isn't working right now? In contrast, a "Seek to Understand" session asks a very specific question: What do we think about a proposal to do X? It's a deep dive to solicit informed feedback on specific ideas or programs under consideration.

For instance, say the leader of a successful business becomes alarmed when he sees how some employees are dressed for work. The ripped jeans and hoodies strike him as out of place. He realizes, however, that multiple factors need to be considered before implementing a policy change. So he decides to conduct a "Seek to Understand" deep dive on the dress code policy.

How does that work? First, everyone invited gets a memo summarizing the issue and any necessary background information, such as links to articles or videos, and his criteria. Everyone has at least a couple of days to reflect on this material. The memo also includes a list of questions that will serve as the agenda for the session.

Try These Phrases

When you're asking your team to discuss an issue, ask them to consider these questions first.

- What specific problem are we solving for?
- How does this relate to our vision and values?
- Can you predict any unintended consequences?
- What would you expect success to look like?
- What clarifying questions should we be considering?

The leader is not laying out a solution but rather a desired outcome. Try to describe it in neutral terms and let people judge it for themselves.

Otherwise, you will be subconsciously pressuring them to agree with your "great idea"—which will cut off authentic feedback and experience sharing.

Another key criterion for a successful Seek to Understand session is that the leader needs to own how the ultimate decision will be made. If you're simply looking for feedback before you make your own decision, that's fine, but you have to say so. Conversely, if you tell people there will be a vote to decide at the end of the session, that vote needs to be binding or you will lose credibility.

One CEO we work with is particularly effective in communicating clearly before a Seek to Understand session. When he asked his executive team for opinions on modifying the company's drug policy, he told them up front: "This is a decision I'm reserving for myself, but your feedback is important to me." That removed any ambiguity. People are usually fine with knowing that their role is to advise rather than to vote—as long as they aren't misled into thinking the team would be making a collective decision.

RUNNING "DISCOVERY SESSIONS" TO LEARN FROM EMPLOYEE EXPERIENCES

If Instant Analysis uses questions to identify pain points for the company, and Seek to Understand uses questions to explore a single new idea, Discovery Sessions use questions to get clarity about the employee experience. We designed them as a structured method of asking people how they feel while doing their daily work, how that experience might be improved, and what they can do to accept responsibility for improving it. These special meetings achieve several valuable objectives:

- They encourage employees to share their experiences.
- They reassure the team that their ideas and suggestions matter.
- They empower the team to make their jobs more efficient and effective.
- They identify development opportunities for the leader and future leaders.

Let me stress that "identifying development opportunities" means that the team is teaching the leader. We don't expect leaders to ask point blank,

"What can you teach me?" but simply to listen carefully to how people describe the company, their work, and their day-to-day environment. Listening will provide important clues to the issues on people's minds while sending a powerful message that you are authentically interested in their experiences.

When done correctly, Discovery Sessions empower employees to make their own changes in how work is getting done. This can scare leaders sometimes and provoke questions like: *What if they do something wrong? What if they screw something up? What if their changes make me look bad?* You will have to push past those fears of looking bad and other ego "stories."

Discovery Sessions sometimes follow an employee survey that includes questions about experience and engagement. Many organizations conduct such surveys with the best intentions, yet most do them in ways that have significant *unintended consequences that decrease buy-in.* They see only the positives about employee surveys: people appreciate being asked about their opinions, and data about the employee experience can be used to monitor and measure trends.

So what can go wrong? Plenty. Asking people to share their opinions causes them to assume that problems they flag will be addressed in the wake of their sharing. If nothing at all is done about such problems, trust or buy-in (or both!) will erode. And if the survey is repeated the following year, cynicism will spike even further.

Here's what usually happens: The executive team gets the survey results and holds a closed-door meeting about how to address them. Are there any burning issues? Let's have a task force come up with a plan to address them. Or let's ask HR to come up with a plan for review. Either way, there's no follow-up questioning for employees to elaborate on the issues raised in the survey. Management just assumes they understand what the results mean, when in fact they might have no idea, because survey questions are often ambiguous. Guessing what people really meant by their answers can be like throwing darts at a target with a blindfold on.

Let me give you an example. When a team member says, "We need more feedback," what does that mean? Do they want feedback on their individual performance, or the company's results? If their own performance, what aspects? And do they mean every week? Once a month? And in what format: Via email? Voicemail? Team huddle? Private coaching session? Any of these are possibly what they intended but couldn't say when responding to an ambiguous survey question.

The gold standard question at the end of an employee survey is typically: "Would you recommend this as a place to work?" HR people call this the "net promoter question." The percent of employees who say, "Heck yes, great place to work!" minus the percent who say, "Run away as fast as you can!" is called the net promoter score.

The Gallup Institute has tracked this score for years at many hundreds of thousands of companies. Are you surprised to learn that the average US company has a net promoter score of only about one-third? In other words, the vast majority lack buy-in and wouldn't recommend their employer to others. Gallup reports that organizations with higher net promoter scores enjoy more profit, better customer service, better safety records, and lower turnover rates.

Like Gallup, my firm surveys thousands of employees across the country, asking whether the respondents would recommend their employer as a place to work. But we go even deeper, exploring nuances that differ across different departments and different locations within the same company. We've learned some interesting data along the way. There's a strong correlation between whether people plan to stay at least another two years and whether someone would recommend the company as a good place to work. The bottom line? An employee's plan to stay indicates buy-in!

Unforced turnover costs tens of thousands of dollars per position at the typical organization, including the time and expense of recruiting, sorting through resumes, scheduling interviews, evaluating candidates, making offers, onboarding, and training. The hidden cost is the aggravation and stress among those who must pick up additional responsibilities for people who quit, while a position is being filled. Productivity also drops when valuable time is spent training new people.

On the flip side, there's also a strong positive correlation between believing "This is a good place to work" and feeling like management really listens to employees and responds to their concerns. People who feel unheard, on the other hand, strongly believe the company is not a good place to work at all. That's why mishandling employee surveys is even worse than never doing them at all.

This isn't to imply that every decision at a company requires input from everyone. That would be pure chaos. But we've found that there are hundreds of decisions made every day about how work gets done that might benefit from the thoughts of the people doing the work. This does not mean that everyone's ideas have to be accepted, merely that everyone's thoughts are solicited and seriously considered.

Discovery Sessions are also a powerful tool to explore issues on the "what's not working" list. The exact same process will allow the team to use Collective Genius to identify the specific issue, prioritize, identify potential solutions, and select what's most impactful to do first. Let's explore how that works.

How to Run a Discovery Session

With the stakes so high, it's worth going into some detail about how to run an effective Discovery Session. We recommend doing them in groups of three to seven people from the same team, facilitated by the team leader, supervisor, or manager. The group should proceed through these phases of understanding an engagement survey:

- Pull three to five questions from the employee survey for a deeper discussion about what people were thinking when they responded. If you're not sure which would be most valuable to discuss, look for questions that provoked the most disagreement, which can be a red flag for ambiguity. For example, someone's response to "My opinion counts in how we get things done around here" is open to many interpretations, based on how they define "counts" or "get things done."
- For each question you have pulled from the survey, follow a simple formula:

    1. Ask each participant to consider silently what people might have been thinking about when they answered the way they did. This taps into the reality that every person will see a well-formed question differently based on their own experience.
    2. Form small groups for people to compare answers and identify possible causes for the answer people gave. Small groups allow every person's thoughts in a larger group to be heard!
    3. Reconvene as a large group and share findings. Take notes

on a flip chart or whiteboard using the exact words the group expresses. If the scribe generalizes or editorializes the original verbiage, people will feel unheard.

- When all issues and problems are listed, participants vote on the ones that would lead to the biggest positive impact if addressed. We typically give people three votes each that they can distribute anywhere they want—either all three on one item or spread around. One caveat: issues that are outside the group's control should be placed on a separate list; it is a fool's errand to ask team members to solve issues beyond their control, for which they may lack relevant information. This separate list becomes the responsibility of the leader to follow up on and report back to the group what they learn.

- Starting with the top vote-getter, ask the team to quickly check in on the criteria for a great solution. Then ask each person on their own to brainstorm potential solutions. If you have more than five or six people, break into smaller groups to brainstorm in parallel. Then record all suggestions, again with no judgment. (Ideas that are outside the control of the team go to a parking lot for follow-up in another setting.)

- After all potential solutions are heard, the group can vote on which ones are the highest priorities. The votes would be an answer to the question "As you consider this list, what solution that's in our control to implement would move the needle the most?"

- Finally, ask for two volunteers to commit to creating a plan with specific steps, timeline, and measures. The team then reviews the proposal at a follow-up meeting or via email for comment. After commenting, owners are assigned to key action steps and the implementation begins!

- In future meetings, celebrate progress and solutions that have been implemented and continue working on the prioritized list, until the group feels the list is exhausted.

- It's important to keep doing Discovery Sessions on a regular basis because the business is always changing with new customers, processes, pricing, challenges, competitors, and so on. If the leader makes this process a "one and done," it can be more damaging than never doing a Discovery Session at all. Additional Discovery Sessions do not require additional surveys. The original prioritized list of issues typically provides months of opportunity. Then, every quarter or so, ask what should be added to the list. Team confidence will build as they experience being entrusted with creating solutions.

Please note that Discovery Sessions are *not* the appropriate venue for the team leader to suggest solutions, pass judgment on ideas, or volunteer to implement solutions. They are all about encouraging people to draw on their own experiences and share why they think things are the way they are and how to make them better. If you want to empower your team, increase buy-in, and improve your net promoter score, you will have to resist any temptation to jump in and take over the process. This is not your show; you are simply the facilitator and notetaker. However, if you feel you have to add a potential solution, offer it after everyone else has spoken and make it clear it's just another idea for consideration.

RESISTANCE TO QUESTION-BASED LEADERSHIP

The leadership techniques we've been discussing in this chapter contradict traditional command and control management, which many executives with lots of experience were trained to practice (including me!). Even when some of those leaders try to empower their people, they find it hard to maintain a more modern mindset.

For instance, a few years ago I was told about a town hall meeting with executives of a large global company, held at an auditorium near their head-quarters. According to the story, the founder and CEO delivered an update on the company's results and challenges, then opened the floor for questions. One leader stood up to ask about the company's travel policy. The CEO reportedly yelled back, "That's the stupidest @#&% question I've ever heard!" There were no further questions from anyone in the auditorium.

In my experience, leaders don't come out and say they don't want to listen to their people. The resistance is usually framed as a matter of time and priorities. For instance, when I urge my clients to run Discovery Sessions, I'll often hear something like, "Interesting idea, but my plate is already full and I don't have time to do another meeting with employees. And my people are just as busy. We don't have the luxury of dropping everything to brainstorm ways to change things."

As a former corporate executive, I know that the idea of holding Discovery Sessions can seem overwhelming. "Where will we ever find time?" we hear overburdened leaders worrying. But of course there's really no such thing as time management, only priorities management. We all have the same amount of time per day; the question is what we consider important enough to do with that time.

All the leaders at one company we work with were working hard, but they had high turnover and negative net promoter scores. The chronic loss of good people was causing huge stress among the remaining employees, and their customers were frustrated by being repeatedly handed off to new account representatives. The company also faced cost overruns due to continuous recruiting, re-recruiting, and training.

The irony is that while the leader at one location insisted he was too busy to do Discovery Sessions, one reason he was so busy was that he was constantly sourcing, hiring, and training new talent. I explained that most of the time he was using to cope with turnover could be redirected to getting his employees engaged, showing them that their voices count, and giving them more control over how work gets done. Sure enough, less than six months after they started Discovery Sessions, turnover dropped by a third and their net promoter scores increased by over 30 points!

WHAT HAPPENS WHEN YOU EMBRACE QUESTIONS?

Fortunately, the question-based techniques in this chapter have a great track record of success. This success is rooted in the fact that the solutions are created not by the leader, but by the people doing the work who will be responsible for its successful implementation!

It's a stereotype that large companies are slow and bureaucratic and that their people lack buy-in. That's not the case at GE Aerospace.[1]

Management received training to connect each employee to strategic and departmental goals and to ask frontline people, "What can we do better?" One huge success from this effort was reducing the time to build helicopter engines from 75 to 11 hours. Imagine the savings from asking questions and empowering people to make changes!

But this is not a technique that benefits only large companies. At the multi-state automotive retailer Jerry Seiner Dealerships, for instance, repair technicians identified smarter ways to do oil changes. Instead of walking over to the parts department, standing in line, telling the parts clerk what they needed, signing for the parts, then walking back to the shop floor, the techs reinvented their workflow during Discovery Sessions. Under the new plan, the company supplies the most commonly used oil change parts on the repair floor, allowing technicians to skip the line at the parts desk altogether. That meant fewer steps, less hassle, and higher productivity for each technician.

You might scoff that any one of the techs could have come up with that plan and presented it to the dealership's managers, and that's true in theory. But without the invitation of a structured process that asked for new ideas, the new workflow was far less likely to be proposed. The highly capable managers at Seiner were always interested in better ways to do things, but the reality of the daily grind was that customers always required attention, immediate problems urgently needed fixing, and everyone was too focused on hitting the monthly sales goals to think about process improvements.

One of my favorite examples of the power of questions comes from Brandon K., who attended one of our leadership training programs a few years ago. He looks like a Hells Angels biker (towering height, solid build, long gray beard), but he's actually quiet, thoughtful, and a well-respected leader at his company. He relayed a story about how he applied question-driven leadership to help his son-in-law, Jack, who was a new manager at the time. Jack had a direct report who was constantly bugging him for a raise, but Jack didn't want to show favoritism over his other people. So he asked Brandon for advice on how to respond.

Most managers try to deflect these situations by kicking the can, perhaps by saying, "We can discuss a possible raise after you achieve X," or, "You are not eligible for a raise for another six months." Such stalling techniques rarely satisfy the employee, and they ignore a potentially valuable opportunity for the leader to gain insight.

Brandon advised his son-in-law to ask his direct report a simple question: "What would getting a raise do for you? What would it allow that you don't have or can't do now?" You might think this question is unnecessary because everyone wants more money for the same reasons, perhaps to buy a nicer car, or satisfy a spouse with better vacations. But people are complicated, and you can't assume motivations. Sometimes you just have to ask.

In this case, the employee replied that the issue was movies. He and his girlfriend were movie nuts who loved to go every weekend, but all those tickets and popcorn buckets were eating up too much of his income. Armed with this insight, Brandon's son-in-law went to the CEO of this small company and got permission to buy the employee a subscription plan at the local theater, with two tickets per weekend. This way no one else would feel that the timing of raises had gotten unfair, while the movie fan was delighted and very grateful. With just a simple question and a modest expenditure by the company, he was bought in!

This relates to a technique we covered earlier: the power of asking, "What's the real issue here?" In this kind of situation, it's easy to assume or guess what's going on, but it's far more powerful to ask and find out for sure. Maybe the solution is easier than you think.

PUTTING ALL THESE QUESTIONS INTO DAILY PRACTICE

If you choose to start a new process like Instant Analysis, Seek to Understand, or Discovery Sessions, be very clear with your team that their active participation is essential to the success of the exercise. You can explain that you've seen the light about the importance of asking good questions and truly listening to their answers. But in return, you're counting on them to be honest and forthcoming. You don't want to end up like the CEO in that silent auditorium.

It may take you a while to practice listening to ideas and suggestions without judgment, without snapping, and without imposing your own strong opinions. Increasing your awareness and hearing yourself as you actually sound to your people is the first step. If you mess up and judge an idea instantly and harshly, all is not lost. You can catch yourself, apologize, and try again. Over time, you can replace your habit of snapping with a habit of thoughtful, nonjudgmental listening.

As you change your leadership style to focus more and more on questions, be sure to take time to celebrate. Thank people for their input. Congratulate them on taking responsibility for new initiatives. And point out the likely impact: less turnover, less wasted time required to hire and train new people, and an overall increase in morale and buy-in. Those are the ingredients of consistently better overall results.

Ideas Worth Considering

1. What decisions should only be made by you as a leader? What's the best way to solicit input from others on that decision and clearly indicate your intent to make it on your own?
2. Healthy, high-performance teams are able to consider issues their colleagues bring forward without needing to provide "the solution." If your team is not accustomed to the practice of hearing issues for feedback (not decisions) from colleagues, what could be done to encourage this?
3. When someone brings you an issue, in what cases should you tell them what to do instead of asking questions?

Chapter 7

PRIORITIZE THE FEW THINGS THAT REALLY COUNT

Not long ago I got a call from an exasperated senior executive at a rapidly growing company: "We got a little bit done on twenty things this quarter, but we only completed one or two. My team feels like they're on a treadmill with no end in sight. They're getting burned out. What do we do?" He explained that each priority made sense on a stand-alone basis, and there were business pressures to get them all done. But attempting to get them all done was clearly not working.

This is a common problem. I've been there and shared the frustration. So much work yet so little accomplished! Any business leader can easily feel overwhelmed by a flood of new information about customer behavior, the supply chain, the labor market, competitors, the economy, and their industry ecosystem. It can be extremely difficult to sort through all that information to set priorities, so many leaders default to creating an "infinite to-do list" of everything they want to get done.

That kind of list can easily become another killer of morale and buy-in. People hate floundering in confusion about what's really important for the organization. As one leader told me, "The bosses keep asking us to do more and more, and it's impossible to get it all done!" The frustration of working long hours yet still feeling like a failure takes a huge emotional toll.

Another hit to morale and buy-in occurs when leaders shift priorities within a quarter in a well-intentioned effort to respond to what's most important. Imagine you were halfway through accomplishing a priority only to receive a new one. How frustrating! This "new, new thing" continuous reprioritization should only be done if there is a crisis. And if crises happen regularly, there is a much bigger problem at play.

The lack of prioritization or continuous shifting of priorities actually creates more work as it increases turnover. According to a Microsoft survey of thousands of workers across nearly a dozen countries, people are seven times less likely to look for another job when they have clear priorities at work. Sadly, only about a third of employees say they receive guidance from their managers about prioritization.[1] In other words, a failure to establish clearly defined and articulated priorities is directly driving higher turnover.

This chapter shows how to sort through the noise and create a very short list of priorities that will spare your team from those problems, while fostering improved motivation, alignment, and buy-in.

WHAT'S THE MAGIC NUMBER?

What's the ideal number of big priorities for an organization to tackle at any one time? While some experts suggest capping such a list at ten or seven or five, I'd go even further: three priorities is ideal. Beyond three, the more priorities you try to set, the more likely that people won't remember them all, let alone execute them all. Once you get to seven or more, it stops being a priority list at all—it's just a wish list.

This principle that "three is greater than seven" is based on how the brain works. It is *much* easier to remember three things than seven, especially in a world full of distractions. This is known as "chunking information," and we see it all the time in daily life. You probably recall your phone number in three parts: three numbers, three numbers, and four numbers. How much easier is that to remember versus a continuous string of ten numbers in a row?

The second piece of brain theory suggests that we more easily remember things that we can relate to something else, like other ideas or images. So, when you offer up a priority, be sure to link it to the purpose, values, or metrics of the company.

Use your team and the Collective Genius Process to generate both the potential priorities list and voting to determine the top three. This will increase their commitment to the priorities—because their voices were heard—and increase the odds of successful execution.

If you can get your people to focus on just three top priorities at any given time, successfully accomplishing them and celebrating them will provide the satisfaction and motivation that become fuel to tackle more. Then new priorities can be added for the next quarter, or the one after.

DO YOU HAVE A PRIORITIZATION PROBLEM?

Here's a simple question to diagnose whether your own organization is having a problem with prioritization. Ask your team to take a minute silently and write down the most important one or two things to get done right now when they consider the organization as a whole. Then go around the table and share. You might be surprised by what you hear in lack of alignment. And remember, the people sitting on your team are the communicators of what's important to their teams. If the messages being communicated are different, the chances of seamless cross-functional communication are slim.

My firm has interviewed hundreds of executive teams as part of our client onboarding process, and we always ask each person to describe the company's or business unit's strategy. We listen for several indicators of alignment or misalignment:

- Do the executives identify the same core strategy and top priorities?
- Do they use the same words (give or take) to describe those priorities?
- Are the strategies and priorities easy to understand?
- Does everyone have them memorized, or do they need to look them up?
- How many priorities are there? (Three is ideal. Five is pushing the limit. Seven or more is a red flag.)
- Have the strategic priorities been clearly connected to everyone's day-to-day tasks?
- Is every person clear on their role in accomplishing the priorities?

We tend to see several common problems after doing this exercise.

If the leader's description of the strategic priorities diverges significantly from how the team members describe them, that clearly indicates a communication problem.

If key team members don't express the same priorities, it's possible that the strategy has been pushed aside by urgent issues that have come up after the most recent strategy session.

If people quote the overall strategy consistently but interpret it differently, the priorities might be too complex or vague, opening the door to conflicting actions.

Failure of strategic alignment is so common that around 80% of the time, leaders we interview use very different language to describe the same strategy, or even describe different strategies altogether! The common result of these conditions is that the odds of employee buy-in drop dramatically. Getting everyone pulling in the same direction will be extremely difficult.

The folks we interview are usually smart and competent at their jobs, but they get overwhelmed by facing an overly expansive to-do list. In the past they would feel hopeful after a leadership retreat where they identified a handful of priorities. But then, inevitably, the new strategy quickly gets derailed as day-to-day issues pile up and the need to hit short-term metrics trumps everything else.

There has to be a better way to sort through the noise, create a very short list of true priorities, and—equally importantly—get that very short list embedded into everyday activities at all levels of the organization and in all departments.

CREATING A PRIORITIZED LIST THAT STICKS

The action plan that follows is not rocket science, but it will take determination and commitment to apply it and stick to it. Your people will need to develop muscle memory to avoid falling into prior bad habits that wreck prioritization. But if you get good at this process, your organization will enjoy the huge advantages that stem from aligning smart strategies with a compelling purpose. You will see the power of clearly communicated, internalized, and executed priorities to drive buy-in at all levels.

This proven process has five distinct steps that build on each other. You'll recognize the first two from chapter 4 on the Collective Genius Process:

1. Ideation
2. Ranking
3. Simplification
4. Clarification
5. Internalization

Ideation simply means generating ideas for consideration. The magic here is using the Collective Genius Process so that everyone contributes ideas.

Ranking is easy to understand but often hard to do. It requires leaving an idea on the table for another time. It doesn't mean the idea for prioritization goes away; it's just not for right now.

Simplification is another task that sounds easy but can be surprisingly hard. My favorite quote about it is Mark Twain's famous apology: "I didn't have time to write a short letter so I wrote a long one instead." The simpler you can express a strategy, the more likely it is to be remembered and implemented. Combining ideas that are the same is another way to simplify.

Clarification is distinct from simplification, because even a simple priority can be misunderstood or misinterpreted. We see so many teams ask at the end of a quarter or year, "Did we accomplish this priority?"—only to hear, "Well, it's really a matter of interpretation." Priorities that generate buy-in are clear enough not to need interpretation!

Internalization means cascading the message so that everyone from the CEO to the front line truly understands the strategic priorities and considers them in what work to get done. Merely announcing the priorities in emails or at town halls, or posting them on the walls of break rooms, won't be enough to achieve internalization and buy-in.

Ideation	Ranking	Simplification	Clarification	Internalization
• Did you use Collective Genius to get the team's best thinking?	• Did you Weigh the Ox to prioritize?	• Is it memorable and easy to repeat?	• Would someone outside the meeting understand its meaning?	• How will you Integrate it?

Step 1: Ideation

This is the most natural step for most teams. We've all been in brainstorming meetings where we were asked to share ideas that might improve our organization and its results. The problem is that there are several common "gotchas" that regularly hinder or sabotage ideation, both before and after ideas are proposed.

Before you get started, it's crucial to establish clarity and alignment around the ideation process. This can be as simple as asking, "How do we want to do this work together?" If you skip that question, a free-for-all can easily follow, as ideas start flying around without any parameters or orderly sequence.

Instead, give everyone a clear process and stick to it. For instance, you might ask everyone to come prepared with a list of ideas and read each one in order of their preference, before the next person continues. Even better, you can have each person read just one idea on their turn, doing a series of rounds until all ideas are exhausted.

If you are meeting virtually, create a slide with boxes that look like sticky notes where each team member can share one idea. The beauty of using an online tool like Google Slides is that each idea is anonymous, which allows us to dissociate the owner from the idea.

Regardless of which ideation process you choose, everyone on the team will benefit from certainty about how the brainstorming is going to happen, and from knowing that chaotic outbursts will be unacceptable.

In addition to failing to establish a clear process in advance, the second major gotcha is what happens after each new idea is floated. You and your colleagues will be very tempted to start an immediate discussion of the pros and cons of each idea. Even worse than premature discussion is getting pulled into premature judgment. Neither is appropriate or helpful during the ideation phase.

For instance, imagine an ideation session where most new suggestions get a negative response from someone else in the room:

- "That will never work."
- "We already tried that two years ago!"
- "Here's why you're wrong."
- "I don't like that idea."
- "Just to play devil's advocate . . ."

Almost immediately, many in the room will start holding back their ideas for fear of confrontation or harsh judgment. As facilitator, your opportunity is to politely remind the group that the first stage of ideation is not the place for judgment, conversation, or debate. There will be time for that in step 2.

Step 2: Ranking

Remember, we are trying to get down to only three big priorities at any one time. The more you push beyond three, the more you risk misunderstandings, confusion, forgetting, failures of execution, and lack of enthusiasm. Or as David Packard, the legendary cofounder of Hewlett-Packard, famously put it: "More companies die of indigestion than starvation."[2]

Post all the ideas offered where everyone can see them, either in person or virtually. Then ask which ideas are the same so they can be combined.

We suggest that ranking criteria for organization-wide ideas includes how much they will "move the needle" of results and if this one idea is better than the others. It's a simple screen that allows people to use their Collective Genius.

Two different screening questions that teams can use to assist them in ranking the ideas generated in step 1:

1. Will this idea result in a 10% improvement or 10x improvement?
2. How does this idea compare to every other idea we are considering?
3. Is this idea significant enough to be a corporate goal or is it more appropriate for an individual department?

10% or 10x?

This distinction is sometimes referred to as "working *in* the business versus working *on* the business." Given a choice, you should usually prefer the latter. Of course, as smaller teams closer to the front line prioritize their ideas, many more will be in the business versus on the business.

There's nothing wrong with an idea that has the potential to increase revenue up to 10%. Consider a new flavor of coffee at Starbucks, or a new regular flight by Qantas between underserved airports. Those might be fine suggestions that add revenue and profit. But in the context of a giant global company, their impact will only be felt on the margins. These ideas are examples of working *in* the business.

A potential 10x idea, in contrast, will fundamentally change how a product is designed, created, packaged, delivered, priced, or some combination of all of them. It can include adding entirely new product lines or expanding into new geographies. It can also include selling off part of the business or discontinuing certain product lines to focus on better ones. Those kinds of ideas are working *on* the business.

When Starbucks introduced mobile ordering on its smartphone app, customers *loved* how much time it saved them once they no longer had to wait in line to order. After a year, mobile sales accounted for 20% of transactions and Starbucks had gained 28% more reward members, contributing to overall sales growth.[3] That led to a dramatic, fundamental change in business results, as mobile sales now account for nearly a third of all Starbucks sales.[4]

Another 10x idea was when Qantas introduced a permanent "Q-tag" for the luggage of their frequent fliers, encoded with an RFID chip that identifies the traveler. Now, whenever I check in for a Qantas flight, I simply place my bag on the belt—no waiting in line, no printing a bag tag. This saves the airline significantly in terms of labor (fewer hours printing and scanning traditional tags) and waste (all those single-use tags). It also makes frequent fliers like me more likely to stick with Qantas. The Q-tag initiative was working *on* the business.

So, as you begin to evaluate the suggestions that came up during ideation, have your team ask three questions:

- Will this idea create a significant, lasting impact on our results within a few years? "Results" might include revenue, cost savings, customer convenience, product differentiation, productivity, economies of scale, or another critical metric.
- Will the time and effort required to execute this idea be worth it? For a 10% idea, the answer is often "maybe"—while a 10x idea is more likely to be a no-brainer.
- Will executing this idea require collaboration across different departments or disciplines? That's another sign of a high-effort/high-reward 10x idea. For instance, mobile ordering at Starbucks required intense cooperation across store management, IT, training, finance, procurement, and so on.

Remember that ideas on the business that really make significant change are rarely accomplished in one quarter or one year. Identifying the "chunk" of the work to be done in the current period is an important way to make progress toward longer-term goals.

Pairwise Comparison

More than a hundred years ago, the founder of the IQ test created a simple system for comparing ideas. Simply ask: Would you rather do this or that? This is known as "pairwise comparison." As it applies to strategic priorities, I suggest letting team members vote on each one-to-one comparison, and the winner of each vote stays in the running, for now.

Let's look at an example of pairwise comparison in practice. The executives at a newly formed applied research institute at a major public university came to my firm with a "boiled down" list of six priorities for the following year. Under each of the six priorities were three milestones, which were all pretty substantial in their own right. Each was a worthy goal that would, if accomplished, move the organization toward its vision. However, each would also require substantial time and effort to execute.

I quickly realized that this wasn't really a coherent strategy with six priorities; it was a loose wish list of 18 priorities that would be impossible to achieve in full. Even trying to pursue all 18 would lead to chaos, confusion, and the kind of frustration that drives talented people to update their resumes and LinkedIn pages.

Solving this problem required just a single half hour meeting, with little debate and no drama. First we had the team use pairwise comparison to narrow down the six broad categories of priorities, using this pairwise analysis worksheet:

In the chart below, please compare each idea or option listed down the Y axis against each idea or option it intersects across the X axis.

If you prefer the one on the Y axis over the one on the X axis, place a 1 in the appropriate box.

If you prefer the one on the X axis, place a 0 in the appropriate box.

	Fundraising and Partnerships (FP)	Capacity Building (CB)	Athlete Performance (AP)	Research Capability (RC)	Student Impact (SI)	Outreach and Publicity (OP)	TOTAL	RANK
Fundraising and Partnerships (FP)								
Capacity Building (CB)								
Athlete Performance (AP)								
Research Capability (RC)								
Student Impact (SI)								
Outreach and Publicity (OP)								

After everyone returned their sheets, it was easy to total the number of times each topic in the far left column got a vote. We wrote the total mentions in the "total" column and then ranked the totals from first through sixth place. We found that three of the six priorities universally rose above all the other three. This is not to say the others were bad ideas; they simply weren't the most important to get done first. They could wait until the following year. We then repeated the process for the milestones under each of the three top-ranked main priorities. Pairwise comparisons for each set of milestones revealed clear choices reflecting the Collective Genius.

Now the group had three clear, high-priority projects that could reasonably be accomplished in the year ahead. And instead of wasting hours on debates that might have become acrimonious, they did it mostly in silence, with no one getting defensive or lobbying for their pet projects.

Pairwise comparison can also be highly effective when narrowing down which metrics are most important to track. Teams that are evaluated on too many metrics at the same time (often called KPIs or leading indicators) can get tangled up in knots. The rule of three applies here as well: if you ask a person to focus on more than three metrics, you are risking widespread confusion, frustration, and disengagement. Collectively, we find executive teams can focus on 10 to 15 measures in any given year. Use a similar pairwise worksheet to isolate the metrics that truly matter most.

Questions to Consider When Ranking Corporate Goals!

- Will this idea result in a 10% improvement or 10x improvement?
- How does this idea compare to every other idea we are considering?
- Is this idea significant enough to be a corporate goal, or is it more appropriate for an individual department?

Even a well-run outfit like the Young Presidents' Organization once allowed its analytics to expand to 214 different metrics! It was the natural outgrowth of people constantly finding new and interesting ways to gauge YPO's performance. The management team had to hack through that long list, ultimately replacing it with just 15 measures that were worth focusing on and aligning everyone around. Having a manageable list made it much easier for everyone to share clear, common goals.

Step 3: Simplification

If your people cannot remember your strategic priorities and need to look them up when asked, don't blame your people! Blame the priorities, which are almost certainly being expressed with too much complexity. Keep it simple! The fewer words it takes to describe each strategy, the more likely it will be memorized, and the less likely it will be misinterpreted.

We've seen many corporate strategies that are so long or poorly worded, no one can possibly remember them. And even if they do attempt to remember them, they are likely to generalize and paraphrase them through their own perspective. Four people interpreting a strategy through their own lenses can quickly lead to four divergent strategies.

Can you boil your priority down to two simple sentences? How about one sentence? Or a few bulleted words? Can you fit it on a 3 x 5 card without printing in small type? This doesn't mean you won't also communicate the details behind each priority, such as milestone dates, target metrics, and tactics for execution. But those belong in other documents, not in the main communication of your strategic priorities. This is a key to cascading.

I once worked with a team that came up with this strategic objective: "Promote lean principles of operational efficiency and waste reduction while introducing effective processes." Personally, I would struggle to memorize this and would rather have a simple explanation of what's to be done!

I pointed out that they were trying to cram three distinct ideas into one sentence: operational efficiency, waste reduction, and effective processes. They needed to take a step back and figure out what they were really trying to prioritize. As we talked it over, they realized that waste was caused by ineffective processes in design and planning that occur upstream of where the product was made. So they greatly simplified their new objective: "Identify and address the three top root causes of waste, document one process for each, and train each person it affects."

Step 4: Clarification

Imagine an executive team that agrees on an objective of "Increase sales of new products by 8%." Without clarification, the odds of buy-in across the company are slim to none, because there are countless ways to increase sales. For instance, the sales department may start offering customers such deep discounts that each sale becomes unprofitable. Perhaps marketing will accelerate future budgets into the current quarter's spending. Perhaps product managers will add a new feature that customers have been asking for, but raise manufacturing costs in the process. Without more clarity about *how* to reach the goal, this priority will remain frustratingly abstract and may foster conflicting tactics by different departments.

For instance, consider Pacific Lifestyle Homes, a very successful, privately owned homebuilder in the Pacific Northwest. Founder and CEO Kevin Wann built a company that was resilient enough to survive the Great Recession, the Covid pandemic, rising interest rates, and other challenges. Its strategic plan was the result of a thoughtful process that included soliciting powerful feedback from all employees.

When my firm first started working with PLH, they were using an earlier strategic plan that was full of what we call "trapdoor words"—as we discussed earlier, these words are open to varying interpretations. Trapdoor words may signal an intention, but not specific guidance on what to do and not do. Classic examples include *improve, communicate, provide feedback*, and so on. Pacific Lifestyle Homes relied on trapdoor phrases such as:

- Establish unique ways of marketing . . .
- Evaluate and elevate sales training . . .
- Create ground rules for use of AI . . .

Those were all important objectives to their business; the problem was that they were all vague and open to conflicting interpretations. Measuring progress was subjective because lack of clarity was a real problem. Wann led the charge to change the language to provide clarity around the intent of the priorities. The team embraced this and now regularly double-checks for trapdoor words.

The lack of clarity happens all the time in organizations. Suppose the owner of the "elevate sales training" initiative decided to require quarterly refresher training for all sales executives, taking up valuable time on their calendars. Regardless of the quality of that refresher training, the requirement would be likely to stir up resentment rather than buy-in. The sales execs would probably see it as an externally imposed requirement, not something they consented to as part of their own professional development.

The takeaway here is important: strategic priorities that affect more than one individual or department need to be set up in conjunction with those people! You don't necessarily need consensus, but excluding people or their representatives from the process often leads to resentment rather than buy-in. One of the biggest frustrations for any executive is when Team A and Team B each own pieces of the same priority project, but they can't bring it to completion because they can't agree on optimal timing and goals. That's often because one or both teams feel the project was imposed on them, rather than the result of a collaborative planning process.

Step 5: Internalization

The CEO of a successful, multi-thousand employee organization once approached me after a meeting of his peers that I was facilitating. He was proud to tell me that his company had just finished creating a strategic plan, and it had been well received across the organization. He believed they would have strong buy-in for the new plan. Curious, I asked how they had communicated the plan to their large workforce. His answer: a mass email followed by town hall sessions.

I've been humbled in the past by believing that simply communicating an idea was enough to have it received, understood, and acted upon by members of my team. Wow, was I wrong! Looking back, I hadn't done a great job considering all the distractions and competing messages in the lives of the people I was trying to reach.

Based on my own history, I had to warn this CEO that he might want to wait before declaring a successful launch of the new strategy. Many organizations use email and town hall meetings to let people know about such initiatives, only to find that the emails are barely read (let alone remembered), and the town halls leave audiences with glazed eyes and yawns. Though they may increase short-term awareness, such tactics will not achieve buy-in.

Internalization may be the final step in the prioritization process, but it's just as essential as the other four. You might think of internalization as integration. The best way to get buy-in for a new initiative is not via mass communications, such as email blasts and town halls. It's via many small group meetings, in which each leader explains the initiative to their direct reports, who then have an opportunity to ask questions and discuss them with their fellow teammates, not a big room full of strangers.

Such small meetings won't work, however, unless all leaders are fully prepared to conduct discussions with their teams. They first need to understand the strategy in detail, including how it will apply specifically to their team or department, what actions will be expected for implementation, and what metrics will be used to gauge progress and success.

The best way to help leaders internalize is the same as with frontline employees: small group meetings with their own leaders, where they will have an opportunity to ask as many questions as they can think of and provide thoughtful feedback. Picture a cascading series of small meetings, from the C-suite down through VPs and mid-level leaders, until absolutely everyone has the chance to understand, internalize, and achieve buy-in.

PULLING IT ALL TOGETHER

For an illustration of how all five steps work together, consider the experience of Jeremy Levitt when he became CEO of Movement Climbing, Yoga & Fitness, a chain of climbing, yoga, and fitness studios. The company was underperforming after being assembled from a merger of three previously independent businesses. The private equity firm that owned the company expected a rapid turnaround. But when Jeremy walked into his new job, he found that everyone seemed to lack clear direction. As he explained during our interview, "Every department was doing what they thought was best, which is not the worst thing in the world, except that they often conflicted with each other."

A different CEO might have immediately put forward their own plan, or pulled one together with just a small team in the corner office. But Jeremy knew that even if he had great ideas, they wouldn't be executed without widespread buy-in. "Whenever you are in a multi-unit business, there's potential for an 'us-versus-corporate' mindset, driving internal rivalry and conflicts. But when you're being listened to, even if you're at the bottom rung, there's a different feeling around your place in the organization."

To give everyone a sense of influence and a stake in the company's future, Jeremy commissioned a SurveyMonkey poll of all 2,000 employees. The questions were open-ended to solicit suggestions to make things better. (*Step 1: Ideation.*)

Then Jeremy assigned leaders to review and prioritize the thousands of suggestions that flooded in. This group narrowed them down to a much more manageable set of about 15 proposals. The results were shared at an executive team off-site meeting, where a wider group could add their own input and further narrow down the list of ideas that would really move the needle. (*Step 2: Ranking.*)

At that same off-site, the executives then discussed how to turn the highest priority initiatives into actionable plans and realistic metrics. (*Step 3: Simplification.*) They also discussed language to discuss the initiatives in ways that mean the same thing to everyone in the company. (*Step 4: Clarification.*)

Next came communicating the new priorities and action plans to the entire organization. Jeremy used a cascading process to explain the initiatives via each employee's direct manager, from the C-suite to the front lines. People had a chance to ask questions in small groups, without the intimidation factor of a giant town hall meeting. That made it easier to absorb what was expected of them. (*Step 5: Internalization.*)

Ultimately, Jeremy was very happy with the degree of employee buy-in for the new initiatives. Employees felt like they had a stake in them, because they had been asked to make suggestions and those suggestions were taken seriously. I've found that in any group setting, when people feel that their perspectives have been heard and considered, they are much more likely to buy into an idea—even if it's not the one they supported. This is another example of the important principle we discussed in chapter 2: "Done with, not done to!"

There's no shortage of good ideas in corporate America. Sadly, however, there is a shortage of leaders who are willing to listen to ideas from the front lines, prioritize the few that have the greatest potential, and then support as many people as possible to run with those ideas as if they were their own.

That's the path that leads to buy-in.

Ideas Worth Considering

1. How do we monitor how well our front line understands our strategic priorities? How many times are they referred to each month for the average employee?
2. What is the process for keeping strategic priorities front and center for your teams? How do you refer to them effectively without getting dragged down into solving for them instead of with them?
3. Consider your strategies as they are currently written. Are there any trapdoor words? How else could we provide additional clarity?

Chapter 8

SLOW DOWN TO INCLUDE EVERYONE

The trailblazing entrepreneur was beside himself. He had moved his com-pany into "first class" office space as one of many efforts to get ahead in an emerging industry. One hot summer day, the power went down—without any signs of when it would be restored. He started to panic. Without backup power in his new office space, he couldn't provide service to his customers. As the minutes ticked by, he feared his hard-won customers might move to a competitor. In a moment of anger and frustration, the entrepreneur picked up a chair and threw it through an upper story window, then strung an extension cord to a working outlet on the ground floor. He'd deal with the consequences of the shattered window later.

That's an extreme example of the impatience felt by many business leaders, especially by startup founders. They don't want to settle for delays or mediocrity. They want everything done right, and done immediately! This drive and energy can be hugely valuable in some circumstances—but at other times it can cause much bigger problems than a shattered window.

Simply put, if you make speed your top priority, you will be tempted to exclude your people from key processes and decisions. And that will ultimately slow you down in the long run, even if it solves some problems faster in the short run. It's a paradox that trips up many leaders: sometimes the best way to grow faster is to *slow down to include everyone*. It's to invest some extra time now for the sake of developing more engaged team members who will ultimately make better decisions and take your company to the next level. If you want to save yourself time for the really important stuff—and get better long-term results—you need to use more time *now* to foster buy-in.

Whenever I tell my clients or audiences that involving more people in getting stuff done will actually *create* time, the usual reaction is eye-rolling and audible groaning. I know this isn't what successful, amped-up leaders like this entrepreneur (or me back in the day) want to hear! However, we have seen time and again that when leaders let go and learn how to effectively involve others in getting stuff done, the result is more time for the leader to focus on high-impact work that will pay off with better business results.

Of course, there are exceptions and times when there is no time to wait. One memorable story is from the tragedy of 9/11. A 25-year-old Air National Guard pilot was on duty when the emergency call came in. The orders were something you never wanted to hear: shoot down the United Airlines jet full of passengers that had been hijacked and was heading toward Washington, DC.

The F-16 jets were ready to scramble until they heard there was a 45-minute wait for the missiles to be loaded onto the jet. By that time, the United jet would already be in Washington. So the young pilot, Lt. Heather "Lucky" Penney, decided to fly without missiles and use her jet to ram into the airliner to bring it down. The F-16 took off, but before it could reach the target for this suicide mission, passengers on Flight 93 had fought the hijackers and caused it to crash.[1] Penney turned around unharmed and would later serve two tours of duty in the Iraq War.

Fortunately, few of us will ever face an extreme situation like that. Day in and day out at work, there is almost never such urgency, except that which we create in our minds. That's why this chapter is about developing the patience and tactics to bring your people along, which is key to creating and sustaining a fully bought-in and motivated team. It's about document-ing and categorizing what needs to get done, deciding who is best equipped to do it, and then preparing them to execute.

There are three elements to the "Slow Down to Speed Up" process:

- Delegating tasks to the right people
- Preparing team members to take on change
- Repeating priorities frequently and clarifying roles

Each idea builds on the others to create a leadership framework to drive buy-in and game-changing results. Let's consider each in turn.

DELEGATING TASKS TO THE RIGHT PEOPLE

What does effective delegation look like? Everyone gives lip service to the importance of delegating, but the devil is in the details: Delegating what? To whom? When? How? If you don't have good answers to those questions, it's easy to give up and say, "Screw it, I'll just do everything myself." And then you're trapped on the hamster wheel of burnout and dysfunction.

The leaders we work with tend to be focused, hard charging, and highly competent. Each has their own ideas about what's most important to get accomplished on any given day. But these ideas often go out the window when they collide with the reality of incoming demands, placed on them by customers, board members, investors, and employees. Sometimes we hear leaders describe their day as "like trying to sip from a fire hose." That's why effective delegation is so important, not optional.

Yet whenever I ask a corporate audience or workshop about delega-tion, almost everyone agrees that it's important—but few consistently practice it. Here are the most common reasons why, and I bet at least a couple sound familiar to you:

- I'm too busy to delegate.
- My people are too busy for me to delegate more to them.
- I'm afraid to overwhelm them.
- They can't do it as well as I can.
- It takes less time to do it myself than to explain it.

A successful Swedish CEO in charge of a digital media business shared with me that her staff gets frustrated sometimes when she's slow to make decisions. She further admitted that the reason for those delays is because she wants to see and evaluate all the relevant data for every decision, which is hugely time consuming. I asked her what would happen if she kept the three most important decisions for herself and delegated the rest to other members of her team. The very thought made her anxious. But then she began to accept that her reluctance to delegate was holding the entire organization back. Any risk from delegating some of those decisions would be offset by the power of demonstrating her trust and belief in her team members. It would allow them to grow their skills and confidence in a safe environment.

Here's how you can make delegation easier and less scary. First, make a list of all the activities you handle in a typical week. Then circle only the ones that are both A) truly important and B) truly within your wheelhouse as the most qualified person to be responsible for them. Then, everything that's left uncircled is fair game for delegation. Go through those one at a time and ask yourself these questions:

- What skills are required to do this project well?
- Who on the team has those skills? (List all who qualify.)
- What criteria or metrics will define an acceptable outcome and a great outcome?
- What resources does the person who gets this project require? Any additional staff, tools, training, and so on?
- What's a reasonable deadline for completion?
- What are reasonable intermediate check-ins?

Then choose *one* task from your list, pick a qualified person, and discuss the objectives, metrics, resources, deadline, and check-ins. Have the other person repeat back their understanding of what's to be done, what a good or great outcome will look like, and how they are expected to keep you posted along the way. Congratulations—you just set up a truly effective delegation! Instead of just telling this direct report what to do, you left room for them to apply their own experience and ideas in deciding how to accomplish the objective. You made it more likely that this person will grow, improve, buy in, and stick around for the long term.

Once you've tested these steps on your first few delegations, they will get easier and faster. For starters, set a goal for yourself to delegate just one project this way each week. This measured approach will prevent you from feeling overwhelmed by trying to turn into an A+ delegator immediately.

PREPARING TEAM MEMBERS TO TAKE ON CHANGE

The second key to including everyone—and giving yourself more time to focus on what's most important—is to prepare others for taking on more responsibility. To paraphrase Harvard Business School professor John Kotter, the leader's job is to set a vision, do what it takes to get the best from each individual, and prepare them for change.[2] That includes modeling how to prioritize and delegate, especially while simultaneously fighting fires and responding to demands from different constituencies. If you devote all your time to "getting the urgent stuff done," including other people will almost always suffer.

Rarely will any of your people be banging on your door, asking you to help them upgrade their skills and empower them to take on more responsibilities. The initiative will have to start with you, which might be very hard if you've never had the privilege of working for leaders who modeled such behaviors. As Kotter has observed, "Most US corporations today are over-managed and underled." He defined management as bringing order to chaos, while leadership is preparing people and organizations for change.[3]

When I look at an organization's strategic plan, one red flag is if every detail is about the "what" while completely excluding the "who." Meaning, if developing leaders is not listed as an organizational priority in order to scale, it's not likely to be executed well. If you exclude talent development and leadership development in your priorities, how are you going to find the people you need to execute the strategy? You can't scale an organization without scaling its people. If you try, it will either grind to a halt or you'll be forced to bring in a constant flow of new hires, while your current team gets demoralized and people start to leave before they can be laid off. The new hires may feel like shiny new objects for a while, until they, too, get ignored or discarded. You can easily end up in a vicious cycle of underperformance, high turnover, frantic hiring, and chronic lack of buy-in.

So developing your people has to be a high priority in your annual plan, with the resources budgeted to support that goal.

Consider Titan Brands, a restaurant group in Las Vegas that has restaurants with a 4.5 rating on OpenTable. Owners Jeffrey Marks and Scott Frost follow the adage that the experience of the employees becomes the experience of the customers. Jeff's own struggles in childhood and Scott's struggles after becoming wheelchair bound after a 2010 accident have enhanced their empathy for the current struggles of their team members.

For instance, they instituted a wellness check-in for every team member, using a platform called "Lollipop." Several times per week, team members complete a brief digital survey indicating how they are feeling and why. If anyone falls below a specified threshold, Lollipop sends an automatic alert to a supervisor with simple suggestions on how to connect with them. This allows the supervisor to check in with the team member so they can be seen, heard, and understood. This simple tactic recognizes employees as human beings with full lives beyond the restaurant. This has helped create a culture of care and understanding and fosters open communication among management and staff, resulting in increased loyalty and employee retention.

Even well-intentioned leaders who commit to preparing their people for more responsibility get tripped up because they assume that preparing them means "I'll teach them the way I do it and then answer any questions they have along the way." That may sound like a good plan, but it usually results in disengagement rather than empowerment. The way you would handle any given project is based on *your* unique perceptions, skills, and experiences. No one else shares those; therefore, no one else can do things exactly the way you do them. Even if you hire people who remind you of yourself and train them to copy your moves to the letter, you will inevitably be disappointed. They can't copy you exactly because they aren't you! If that's your metric of success, your people will always fall short.

And there's another drawback to trying to clone yourself: the people you develop will inevitably face new issues that you've never faced. It's impossible to give them a comprehensive playbook for every conceivable problem. Instead, you need to teach them how to evaluate new situations, set criteria for positive outcomes, devise multiple possible paths to reach those outcomes, then choose which way to go. Otherwise, if you only expect them to copy what worked before, they will be completely stymied by any situation you haven't explicitly taught them about.

Once you accept the urgent need to develop your people, the next big question is how to do it, and how much time and budget you should allocate for it. Of course, there's no single right way to approach development—you need a plan that will make sense for your unique workforce, industry, and resources. You will have to assess the needs of your people before deciding how best to support their development. Great leaders do this two different ways. First, they observe how their people process challenges, interact, and drive results—and notice where they seem to need the most coaching or teaching. Equally important, great leaders ask each team member to identify the number one skill they want to work on in the coming year, as part of the annual performance review process. Then they ask how their work will change when they master that skill.

We work with some successful organizations that designate a fixed personal development budget per employee per year, depending on each person's level in the organization. Then they give each person the freedom to invest their budget in whatever way they might find most helpful, such as taking outside classes at local colleges or business schools.

Niles Industrial Coatings in Fenton, Michigan, is one of those success stories. The company was founded by the grandfather of current CEO Ryan Niles. The family sold the company when Ryan was young, but the new owners went bankrupt and Ryan bought back shares for pennies on the dollar. Ryan's hard work and focus on people resulted in year-over-year successes. Today they operate in a dozen states and have earned the trust of major customers including Dow, DuPont, and Ford.

Part of that success is Ryan's commitment to growing people to provide even better service to customers. They invest between \$2,500–\$3,500 per year on training and development for each team member. The amount varies based on what the company can afford in any given year. As Ryan says:

When we invest in unlocking the potential of our people, we are empowering them to take on more responsibility. When our team members are given more responsibility, understand their purpose, and can see how their efforts directly impact our success, we have their buy-in. They then take care of the customer, and the customer takes care of the company. It's a cycle that is rooted in an initial investment and an investment as a leader that is so rewarding to witness every day.[4]

Other organizations set up their own internal development programs, creating in-house classes or even entire "universities" to teach key skills that they consider necessary for employees to master. One example of that approach is SME in Plymouth, Michigan. This multi-state engineering consulting firm is led by second-generation CEO Mark Kramer, who commits himself to the development of his 400+ strong team. SME has dedicated in-house leadership classes, conducts engagement surveys to determine areas for further development, hires coaches for executives, and trains cross-functional teams. This attention to people and investment in development is no small part of why SME regularly receives "best place to work" awards. The buy-in attitude of the team shows up in customer experience as well. SME has achieved a remarkable client net promoter score of 82, which rivals those of much larger companies like Nordstrom and Southwest Airlines.

In addition to putting people into formal courses, whether externally or in-house, there are many other opportunities to help team members develop or hone new skills. For instance, you can invite them to join cross-functional teams where they will naturally learn from people in other departments. You can assign them to shadow members of another department that specialize in whatever you want them to learn. Or you can ask them to lead a new project or explore a new opportunity that will naturally push them out of their comfort zone.

REPEATING PRIORITIES FREQUENTLY AND CLARIFYING EVERYONE'S ROLE

The third key to slowing down to speed up is to enable people to integrate the top priorities into their day-to-day work. The work of leadership is so much easier when people collaborate on a common goal. You already know that to work on a common goal requires everyone on a team to understand the goal and to understand their role in achieving it. But are you sure they know it as well as you do with all that is going on?

You'll remember back in chapter 3 two of the five questions that leaders can ask to determine if the people on the front line relate to priorities and how they are measured. The first is, "What are the most important priorities your department or team are working on right now?" The second question is, "Where do the results of your work show up on the team scoreboard (or KPIs)?"

When you ask your team members about team priorities, do you get a blank stare or do they tell you what is on their "to do" list? Or, at the other extreme, are you able to hear people using simple language to describe what's to be accomplished? If so, that does not happen by accident.

It's hard to fault leaders for feeling like they don't have the time to slow down to include everyone in getting clear on the answers to these questions. The demands placed on leaders by customers, their leaders, market changes, cost pressures, and staffing up feel like they leave little time for anything else. Compounding the situation, rarely do leaders' supervisors ask, "Hey, how well do your team members understand their role in priorities for the quarter?"

So how do effective leaders show up in inviting active engagement in priorities and measures?

First, leaders hold sessions to understand from the frontline perspective exactly what is working and not working in terms of getting the job done effectively. This information is used by the team to identify potential solutions that inform departmental priorities.

After priorities are established, the leader shares them with the team and asks team members to think about how they can contribute to successful accomplishment. Then a follow-up meeting occurs where the leaders allow team members to collaborate on how they can contribute toward the quarterly goals.

This collaboration, discussion, and inclusion is in contrast to the old-style leader who would keep the goals to themselves and issue orders to people on what they were to do while keeping them in the dark about what it was contributing toward. Slightly more effective, some leaders would tell people the goals and never ask people to connect to them by identifying how they contribute.

The process is the same for the measures important to the department where someone works. The second question of "Where do the results of your work show up on the team scoreboard (or KPIs)?" identifies if people understand that their work is contributing toward the greater good, including the company purpose. There are several prerequisites for the measure to be successful in generating buy-in.

The first prerequisite is that people need to understand what the measure is, how it's defined, how often it's measured, where to find it on a real-time basis, and why it matters. Next, they need to identify how their own work contributes to that measure.

Five Criteria for Effective Measurement

- Is it a predictor of future results/problems or a lagging/past indicator?
- Is it easily captured or does it take lots of work?
- Does it change frequently enough to indicate trends?
- Taken together, do the measures help assess the health of the business?
- Can it be easily manipulated (or "gamed")?

The leader has multiple opportunities during a quarter to remind the team of the common priorities and call out people's behaviors and choices that contribute to their accomplishment. This reinforcement occurs in regular department meetings, in one-on-one sessions, in team meetings on the factory floor at the beginning of shifts, on Post-it notes and flyers in the break rooms, on team WhatsApp groups, and in celebrations!

THE BUY-IN PAYOFF

Slowing down to speed up seems contrary to the go-go-go demands of today's business. However, if your goal is to scale the organization, it will require honoring people by delegating to them, preparing them for change, and reminding them of priorities frequently.

These techniques will reduce stress in the organization by allowing more people to contribute their experience and education to accomplish what's really important (in addition to the day-to-day work!).

Three Things Leaders Want Every Employee to Know

- **Priorities:** What's the most important for them to complete
- **Measures:** What specific results they need to achieve
- **Purpose:** How the company purpose connects to their work

As we saw in the SME example, there is a direct connection between slowing down to include everyone and the customer experience. This experience from leader to team member to customer is a virtuous cycle that breeds success.

Ideas Worth Considering

1. How well do we train our leaders in the art of delegation? How do we encourage the delegation process to occur and how often?
2. How do we prioritize leadership development? What does it look like in our organization? Is it broadly executed or only for "fast trackers"? How do we measure the results?
3. How effective is our formal process for integrating organization-wide and cross-functional objectives into day-to-day activities?

Chapter 9

BE A CATALYST FOR IMPACTFUL CONVERSATIONS AND EFFECTIVE MEETINGS

The TV station was dominant in their market, with one of the largest local market shares in the country. Having worked in broadcasting myself, I was really curious to get inside as an advisor and see the magic that sustained this success. I was invited to one of the executive team's weekly staff meetings, late in the year. Fourteen people gathered around a long table in the conference room. The agendas were passed out, with the only major item listed very simply: "Next Year's Budget." I could imagine attending as one of the department heads, wondering what would be expected of me with such a vague agenda. I'd probably be extremely cautious, responding to questions if asked but not volunteering.

Sure enough, that's what I witnessed. The CFO summarized how next year's finances were changing from the current year, then solicited questions. One or two executives asked about timing and deadlines, but there were no substantive questions or comments. The meeting wrapped up ahead of schedule.

It struck me that this had been both a waste of time and a waste of human potential. The update from the CFO and the obvious questions could have been covered in writing and distributed in advance. Then a more effective use of the time would have been to frame questions in advance for the group to discuss. For instance:

- Are there ways we can improve the effectiveness of the budget process this year?
- Can we add some best practices to involve our teams in budget creation?
- What are the pros and cons of investing more heavily in X, Y, or Z?

Instead, this kind of meeting was a prime example of how to disintegrate buy-in.

Meetings can fail for numerous reasons, including if the topics are not relevant to the participants, the discussion is poorly managed and drifts into ratholes, people don't understand what's expected of them, and attendees are allowed to let their minds wander—a "lights are on but nobody's home" mindset. Fortunately, all of these problems are fixable, and meetings can be transformed into a great opportunity to generate buy-in.

This chapter applies to both group meetings and one-on-one conversations. It applies to in-person one-on-one meetings and team meetings in person and remotely. In all cases, it's about how we set up a structure (what I call a "container") that drives engagement and brings out the resourcefulness of all participants. Conversations that count are a huge factor in driving higher buy-in, productivity, and (ultimately) profitability.

Let's begin by considering the six factors for building a powerful container that will turn your meetings into a source of insights, ideas, and decisions, while avoiding countless wasted hours:

- Defining a smart agenda
- Adopting a collaborative mindset
- Creating space for best thinking
- Picking the person with the right skills to lead the meeting

- Inviting the right number of attendees
- Ending with honorable closure

DEFINING A SMART AGENDA

If you want people to contribute their experience and insights to an issue, it's necessary to let them know the topic ahead of time and what input you want from them. A successful meeting begins before the meeting with a thoughtful agenda answering those questions. A great agenda always indicates:

- What topics are we addressing?
- How do you want me to participate? Responding to ideas, brainstorming new ideas, or evaluating predefined options?
- What's our goal today: sharing information, engaging in discussions, or reaching decisions?
- How much time are we allocating to each topic?

This detailed agenda and all necessary background materials should be distributed well in advance. There was no reason the CFO at that TV station couldn't have distributed the budget targets versus the prior year, key assumptions, and a timetable well in advance. Then the leaders around the table would have had time to consider what the new budget meant for their areas of expertise, and how they might improve it.

Why Are Most Meetings Ineffective?

When I was newly hired as CEO of an internet company, but before I actually took over, I was asked to attend my first board meeting as an observer. To my surprise, the outgoing CEO told me flat out that his objective was simply to get through these meetings without being told what to do by the venture investors on the board. I was fascinated to read the board package his staff prepared, which consisted of a two-page status report plus more than 100 pages of data, but no analysis of the data.

When I asked why, the outgoing CEO replied something to the effect of: "What I've learned is that my VCs act like they have attention deficit disorder. If I throw a lot of data at them, they will never get around to telling me what to do. One asks a question about page 27, another about page 84, a third about a chart on page 35, and before you know it, they all rush out to catch their flights back to the East Coast."

Not surprisingly, that board meeting my predecessor ran was a waste of time. It was just one of many examples I've seen of meetings that do the *opposite* of fostering meaningful conversations, whether intentionally or not. And I'm far from the only one who thinks most meetings are a waste of time and a motivation killer, whether in person or on videoconferencing. In virtually every survey of white-collar workers, meetings are cited as one of the biggest time wasters. Almost everyone I know hates them, in part because no one these days has time to waste!

The quality of any meeting depends on the effectiveness of the meeting leader, regardless of whether everyone is at home or in a conference room. Any decent meeting is a *conversation*, not a one-way lecture. So if you want to run *great* meetings, you need to figure out how to foster nourishing exchanges that will lead to fresh insights, smart decisions, and improved productivity and greater buy-in.

The Typical Way	The Buy-In Advantage Way
Someone brings up a problem and someone else throws out a solution that others react to.	Align on desired outcomes. Agree on criteria. Allow for individual thought work. List all ideas *before* discussion.
Timekeeping is seen as a hindrance—a "cop."	Allow for all meeting attendees to be responsible for how much time is allocated to a topic and, if extending the time, recognize that it's at the expense of other topics.
Good ideas are brought up and lost in fast-paced conversation.	Use the parking lot as an active document to capture good ideas and set future agendas.
Meetings end because time runs out.	End meetings with a formal process to capture what's been agreed to, next steps, what needs communication, and who is doing what.

ADOPTING A COLLABORATIVE MINDSET

If you want to inspire people to truly show up for a meeting, it's important that you establish the right mindset in advance. A powerful container creates an atmosphere, high expectations, and encouragement for full participation. So many leaders I work with complain that their people come to meetings without energy or enthusiasm, often sitting silently without contributing a single suggestion. But if you're the only one speaking or making suggestions, it's a clear sign that you haven't set up an environment of trust in advance.

Engaging people at the very start of a meeting is an effective technique so they won't get distracted by everything else going on in their busy day. One way to do this is to go around the room and ask attendees to share their expectations before launching into the agenda. You can never be sure what's on people's minds. During one session I ran as a CEO, I quickly realized that the leadership team was so preoccupied by an urgent "fire" they had to put out, they couldn't focus on our longer-term agenda. So there was no sense in forcing people to stick to the original plan. We set aside the agenda until a future meeting, and the team used that hour productively to focus on the fire.

What do you do if expectations come up that you can't address in that meeting, or that you feel would be a mistake to begin to address? It's important to call out an issue that's not realistic as part of your current agenda, and respectfully ask the person who brought up the new issue for an alternative plan to address it. That might be as simple as asking, "Is this something we can add to our next agenda?" Or perhaps, "Can we set up a one-on-one discussion about this?"

At the end of each meeting, refer back to the expectations list and ask the team how well each was addressed. I suggest the check-in method that was used in ancient Rome (or at least the way it was depicted in the film *Gladiator*!). Have your crowd indicate whether the gladiator should live or die. Simply ask the team about how well their expectations were met by showing thumbs up (We did it!), thumbs down (We didn't get to that expectation!), or thumbs sideways (Kind of.).

CREATING SPACE FOR BEST THINKING

Another element of making meetings matter is creating space in your meetings to allow everyone to do their best possible thinking. Such meetings give everyone a voice in solutions and foster buy-in about whatever needs to be done. There are two ways to do so at every meeting of more than two people, whether it's a standing staff meeting, a special topic meeting, or an ad hoc session. These two simple steps to create a safe space are aligning on expectations and connecting as humans before diving into business content.

An opportunity to create buy-in in every meeting is to connect as human beings before diving into "real work." I put that in quotes because connecting as people *is* real work! It makes getting stuff done much easier and more fruitful. My favorite "get on board" question is asking people about an emotion-evoking experience they had in their youth. These experiences create primary belief systems that act as filters to interpret what we see. This helps others understand who they are, how they are wired, and where they came from. The question should be put on the agenda so people may consider their answers in advance. In the meeting, allow everyone just a minute or so to answer. If there are more than six or eight people and you are limited on time, break into small groups or pairs to answer.

What if someone doesn't want to answer or can't think of such an early experience? No problem! Allow them to answer the best they can or pass with no judgment. This is not about prying into anyone's personal life; it's about sincerely wanting to understand each other's experiences as fellow humans. The most effective "get on board" answers reference an emotional experience that occurred before age twelve. In those preadolescent years, we each form the filters that help us interpret the world. A key to understanding someone is to understand their filters. That's why a great question might be, "Tell us about a time growing up when you faced a challenge you didn't expect. How did you overcome it? What did you learn?" So understanding the experiences of our colleagues allows us to understand their perspective as an adult.

Some people use questions like "What's your favorite TV series?" or "What's the last book you read?" These can be interesting, and I'm always looking for feedback and good ideas on programs and books. However, they really don't give me any insight into who people are and what causes them to show up the way that they do. It's nice to know that they also enjoyed *Succession*, but that bit of knowledge won't help me or the rest of the team feel more empathy for the path they've traveled, or help us support them better.

One question we always ask in pre-session surveys: "How comfortable is the team in sharing opinions openly, especially when they sense others may not agree?" The leader, who is generally very comfortable sharing their opinions, is often surprised when almost no one replies with, "All the time, boss!" One team whose average answer was 5 on a 10-point scale told us, "We like each other, we trust each other, we just don't feel comfortable sharing our truth all the time." This team lacks the trust necessary to get their best ideas on the table. This lack of explicit trust had to be overcome before the team could achieve full potential by tapping into each individual's unique experiences.

One often unrealized benefit of having diverse senior team members is the ideas and knowledge informed by their unique experiences. If there is not a safe space to express those, we have left people's potential on the cutting room floor!

As we've seen elsewhere in this book, leaders should always go last—except when it comes to vulnerability. The answer to a "Get on Board" question is a perfect opportunity to demonstrate being vulnerable. It's difficult to be vulnerable if you don't feel safe, so this is also a great chance for the leader to demonstrate that they feel safe. So please go first with your "get on board" answer. How vulnerable you are will set the tone for how safe the space really is.

Get on Board Question Strategies

The "Get on Board" question is an important opportunity to connect people as humans before diving into the work of work! Done correctly, the answers provide insights into what makes people tick and what informs their perspective.

Weak "Get on Board" Questions	Impactful "Get on Board" Questions
Tell us about your favorite movie.	Tell us about a time growing up when you overcame a challenge. What happened? How did it make you feel?
If you could be someone else for a day, who would it be?	Tell us about a time growing up when you did something you were not sure you were capable of. What happened? How did it make you feel?
What are your summer vacation plans?	Tell us about a time growing up when you were asked by an adult for your opinion on an important issue. What happened? How did it make you feel?

If you do more than a meeting a week with the same people, "Get on Board" questions will quickly feel repetitive. In that case, shift to asking a different kind of question whose answers will change from week to week, such as: "Please share one personal thing and one professional thing you're excited about this week." Note that each celebration gives you insight into the respondent and makes it easier for others to help support them. Scan the QR code below to access more Get on Board questions to use with your team.

And if you feel like you've exhausted all emotions, pick an emotion from this feelings wheel[1] and create your own question that gets at that feeling. Anything that gets team members to connect as human beings before they become human doings is great.

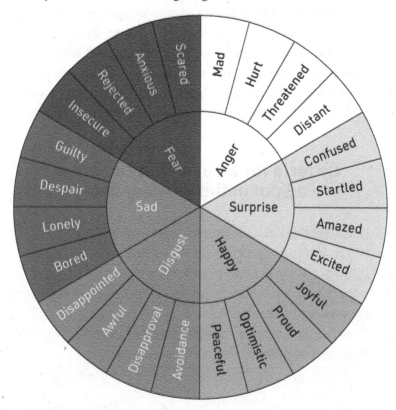

And finally, to allow trust to flourish, it's important for people to be clear on one additional element: a quick discussion of ground rules. This should be repeated whenever there's a new participant in a recurring meeting, so that no one is left guessing about what's expected and appropriate (and not). Setting ground rules usually takes less than three minutes and is simply an answer to the question "What behavior is acceptable and what do we expect from each other?" This should include agreement about the use of smartphones or other devices during the meeting, about sidebar conversations, and about how everyone is expected to participate. The leader should not create these rules—they should be devised organically by the entire team. (Done with, not done to!)

When you create this environment, some ideas will flourish that have nothing to do with the topic at hand. This is where another best practice comes into play: the parking lot. You can simply create a running list of ideas and issues that come up that will need attention, *but not in this meeting*! Without a parking lot, either an idea is skipped over and forgotten "because we don't have time," or the new tangent throws the meeting totally off track from its agenda. A skilled facilitator will allow a new idea to be explored for a minute or two and sense how much energy is in the room about it: Does it excite more than one person? Does it generate conversation? If so, it's worth putting in the parking lot for later discussion.

Criteria for Issues That Deserve a Spot in the Parking Lot

- Is this issue one that requires multiple perspectives?
- Will resolving it impact our future business results?
- Is it important to multiple people in the meeting?
- Is there more information required before having an intelligent conversation or resolution?
- Does this topic deserve separate time that all of us set aside for discussion at a future meeting?

The parking lot becomes a valuable reference document and deserves an owner to manage it and maintain it in an easily accessible online location so anyone can see it and add to it. Some of the topics will be suitable for one-on-one meetings, some for team meetings, some for off-sites. The owner can suggest to the team how and when a topic should be dealt with. Every quarter or so the owner can lead a group discussion to scrub the list of topics no longer relevant.

PICKING THE PERSON WITH THE RIGHT SKILLS TO LEAD THE MEETING

It might seem obvious that before any meeting begins, people need to figure out who should be leading it. Yet, in most organizations, little or no thought is given to this question. By default, the person with the most senior title in the room usually leads the meeting.

The quality of any meeting depends on the effectiveness of the meeting leader, regardless of whether everyone is at home or in a conference room. Any decent meeting is a *conversation*, not a one-way lecture. So if you want to run *great* meetings, you need to figure out who can foster nourishing exchanges that will lead to fresh insights, smart decisions, and improved productivity and greater buy-in.

The executive leading the meeting can inadvertently cause meetings to waste time, because the knowledge, skills, or priorities of the highest-ranking person in the room are not what's required. Instead, the leader of a meeting should be someone who is laser-focused on the agenda, skilled in facilitating group conversation, comfortable calling out when the conversation is going off track, and willing to stop tangents by moving them to a parking lot for discussion later.

The role of timekeeper is not about being a bully; it's about a collective, informed decision of what's most important. It's required to keep the group aware of time and take responsibility for making sure time is being used intentionally. Unintended consequences can be terrible when meetings start late and run over. Some organizations even have a policy of locking the conference room door at the starting time!

When Jeremy Levitt was CEO at Movement Climbing, Yoga & Fitness, he had a "eureka" moment and said to his team, "I just realized I am not the best person to lead our meetings. It's not my strong suit. What would you think if Sarah led the meetings?" The team was surprised by the admission, and Jeremy's vulnerability set the stage for others to be more vulnerable as well. No longer did they need to look like they were perfect at everything, thanks to Jeremy's modeling of recognizing his own strengths and weaknesses.

INVITING THE RIGHT NUMBER OF ATTENDEES

The right number of attendees is an important consideration in creating meetings that matter. The answer depends largely on the purpose and content of the meeting.

If the meeting is about sharing information with no need for discussion or problem-solving, then the meeting can have hundreds of attendees. In the brokerage business they refer to these as "shout-downs," as in shouting information down the line. Most of the time, the attendees half listen while working on other stuff.

If you want a meeting to solve problems or coordinate activities, we use the analogy of a dinner party with clients. How many adults can you have at a dinner party where just one conversation is taking place *and everyone gets to participate*? Whenever I ask that question, the answer is usually about six people. And so it is with meetings. If you want active participation and getting the best thinking on the table, limit attendance to six. "But wait," I'll often hear, "there are others who should know about what we discuss or may have subject matter expertise." That's true, but save everyone time and share with those people what they need to know after the meeting! If there is expertise necessary to inform a discussion, arrange for the person to attend that one meeting or share the information in advance. Having more than six people attend a meeting that is meant to produce results is asking for trouble—a lesson I learned the hard way.

ENDING WITH HONORABLE CLOSURE

There are unintended consequences whenever a discussion keeps going until the last minute of a scheduled meeting and then people run out the door. You'll hear people quickly declare, "Oh, this is great but I've got a call and gotta go!" Or perhaps, "Sorry, I have to get to another important meeting." And then the conclusions are left undefined, and the next steps and action items are left hanging.

There's a better way, which I call "honorable closure." Its purpose is to ensure there is time set aside at the end of each meeting for capturing all the ideas, commitments, and key points raised by participants. If a meeting is really worth having, it's really worth agreeing to what was said, what was agreed on, and what needs to happen next. This should happen at every single meeting with three or more attendees.

To do an honorable closure, the leader simply stops all discussion with five or ten minutes left, then asks questions about such topics as:

- Key Takeaways
- Next Steps / To-Dos
- Cascading Communications
- Process Check
- Rating on a Scale of 1–10

No matter how large a department or organization, everyone knows when an important meeting is occurring. It could be an off-site meeting, a special meeting on an urgent topic, or a visit from owners or headquarters to which only certain leaders are invited. Everyone who wasn't invited will be curious to know what happened.

Unless the people in the meeting make a special effort to agree, the well-intended answers to the question of "What did you all do?" create mistrust. Here's why: when a person in Department A hears their leaders' answers, it's human nature to compare notes with their buddy in Department B. If the message or interpretation of the meeting is different for the two of them, they are each led to wonder what really happened, and what other information is being held back. This causes uneasiness and sometimes downright suspicion.

Fortunately, it's easy to nip this in the bud. Take a minute or two at the end of the honorable closure and decide one simple sentence that everyone in the room will say when asked about the meeting. For example, if it's an off-site, the answer might be, "We worked on planning for next year and learning new leadership tools." And then if someone asks what the new plan is, simply add, "We have more work to do, but when the plan is ready to share we look forward to getting your reactions and ideas."

MEETINGS DON'T HAVE TO SUCK!

You often hear that business meetings are mostly a waste of time. Anytime employees are letting their hair down, they are likely to complain about meetings that are just "death by updates" or that devolve into back-and-forth "tennis match" debates between just two attendees, while others can only watch, zone out, or fume about the time they could have been spending on useful work instead. You can't blame a remote format for "Zoom fatigue"—the same skills that foster good conversations in person can also work remotely.

Now you have the tools for a thoughtful agenda that will provide intent, clarity, and expectations. You're providing enough information ahead of time to allow team members to show up fully prepared and ready to share and discuss their best thinking. You have a plan for who's going to lead the meeting and how it will stay on track. And you have a structured discussion format that can turn even routine meetings into action-oriented conversations that add real value. That's the buy-in approach to great meetings!

Six Factors for Powerful Meetings	
Define a Smart Agenda	• Define Topics • Share How to Participate (Responding to Ideas, Brainstorming, Evaluating Predefined Options) • Indicate Our Goal (Share Information, Discuss, Decide) • Allocate Time per Topic
Adopt a Collaborative Mindset	• Ask for Expectations at the Beginning • Revisit Expectations at the End
Create Space for Best Thinking	• Connect First as Human Beings (Get on Board Question) • Establish Ground Rules
Choose a Leader with Process Skills	• Identify the Best Person for Facilitating Discussions (May Not Be the Team Leader) • Select a Timekeeper Responsible for Making Sure Time Is Used Intentionally
Invite the Right Number of Attendees	• Select a Small Group of Attendees (Ideally No More Than Six)
End with Honorable Closure	• Recap Key Takeaways • Confirm Next Steps / To-Dos • Agree on Cascading Communications • Conduct a Process Check • Rate the Meeting on a Scale of 1–10

The simple tools we've just covered will transform meetings from time wasters into effective and efficient engines of mutual understanding, idea generation, effective decision-making, alignment, and buy-in. The best part is that these tactics cost nothing except a little time and a commitment from team leaders. Whether you're responsible for a meeting of 3 or 300, in person or virtually, success starts with adopting an intentional mindset, scripting the flow, and creating space for best thinking by soliciting expectations and connecting as human beings.

With relatively little effort, you can turn humdrum sessions into productive meetings that inspire, engage, and leave people feeling motivated, supported, and part of a team effort worth making!

Ideas Worth Considering

1. Are all of our meetings necessary? Are there any meetings that are primarily information exchanges that could be done in writing more effectively?
2. How do we decide who leads a meeting? What are the characteristics we are looking for in a great meeting leader?
3. Is there a format we would like to adopt that contains new meeting elements to make meetings more effective? How do we best equip meeting facilitators to put these into practice?

Chapter 10

DEFINE A PURPOSE AND VALUES THAT PEOPLE TAKE SERIOUSLY

Most organizations have unknowingly missed the opportunity to create a powerful North Star that can be used every day to create a Buy-In Advantage culture. In fact, what most leaders (including me!) have learned or been told about purpose and values applies to the workforce of the early 2000s and is no longer relevant. Even organizations that have checked the box in creating purpose and values rarely use them to their fullest impact to create game-changing results.

Consider your own organization: How many times in the last week has a member of your team referred to company purpose or values in hiring, promotions, evaluations, or decision-making? When people refer to your purpose, do they see themselves in it and have a sense of energy?

Purpose is used in Buy-In Advantage organizations to help choose between different priorities: Which one will get us closer to our purpose more effectively? Values are used in Buy-In Advantage organizations to inform decisions: How do each of these alternatives best fit our values?

This chapter is about a new way to rediscover the organization's purpose and values for today's workforce and how to apply them in every-day practice. In a healthy workplace, purpose and values known and used by all are the twin drivers of the culture.

PURPOSE IN THE BUY-IN CULTURE

Making money, market share, and return on investment (ROI) can never be part of a healthy organization's purpose. Making money for the share-holders or other investors is a business goal—and an important one—but it's not going to motivate employees. Even Sam Walton, one of the most driven and successful capitalists of the 20th century, understood this. His original vision for Walmart was that the chain would help customers "reduce the cost of living." This was later translated into the advertising slogan "Save Money. Live Better." And when Sam spoke about the vision of saving money for his customers, his crystal-clear authenticity let everyone know what they were doing was making a difference in others' lives.[1]

Another problem leaders face around purpose is that they get the concept confused with mission and goals. *Purpose* (sometimes also called vision) answers the question of *why* something is worth doing. *Mission* is how an organization sets out to accomplish its purpose. *Goals* are how accomplishing the mission will get done in a certain period of time. *Measures* are indicators of success or failure in what's getting done.

WHY PURPOSE REALLY, REALLY MATTERS

With the popularity of *Start with Why* and similar books, many business leaders are aware that identifying a purpose beyond profit is important.[2] Up until recently, however, that awareness was generally seen as optional or secondary, instead of as an essential element that informs strategies for company growth. In our post-pandemic world, it is now a "must-have." When done correctly, it becomes a go-to source to reorient and inspire team members.

As we referenced earlier, two different forces have accelerated the importance of purpose over the last few years. One, the Covid pandemic, allowed many to get their work done in different places and reclaim time that was previously spent commuting. It also gave people a rare opportunity to step back and rethink what's truly important and how they wanted to devote their energy.

The second accelerator is generational. The millennials are one of the largest generations in American history and will continue to dominate the workforce for years. They generally see purpose as very important to their work—especially as they now enter middle age. After age 40, according to German psychologist Erik Erikson, most people's *personal* identity shifts more toward how we contribute to the world.[3] Interestingly, Generation Z, which will soon represent a quarter of the workforce, has a slightly different take on purpose. Research suggests that for Gen Z, the importance of purpose in organizations is understanding how they contribute (or not) to social issues.[4] This places an increased emphasis on values.

Every succeeding generation will have different nuanced needs and expectations. What I believe will not change is a desire to contribute and be heard.

Purpose is not only more important than ever; it has to pass the hurdle of being compelling. In other words, company purpose can't be a trite saying generated in isolation by the CEO or quickly decided by a few for the many. Aiming to be "the best" or "number one" or "market leaders" doesn't cut it anymore. Going through the motions and "checking the box" on a purpose is more damaging than not expressing one at all. Leaders are constantly being evaluated on their authenticity and human connection toward their people, even if those judgments are never expressed out loud.

Research by McKinsey & Company highlights three pieces of data that connect purpose to buy-in:

- Eight out of ten employees say it's important that their company has a purpose.
- Two-thirds say their own purpose is defined by their work.
- Over 90% say they are likely to recommend their workplace to others *if they are inspired by the purpose.*[5]

In other words, purpose is no longer a *nice-to-have* for organizations that want to compete for and retain the best talent. A compelling purpose is a *must-have*. If two-thirds of employees say their own purpose is defined by their work, that implies that ignoring purpose will alienate that majority and create a turnover issue.

WHAT PURPOSE IS—AND WHAT IT'S NOT!

Purpose is the reason your work is worth doing. Purpose is the source of motivation to go the extra mile, to work long hours when required. It describes how the world is different because the organization exists and is therefore emotionally compelling.

A generation ago, eyebrows might have been raised if someone were asked the purpose of their organization. "To make money, of course!" you might have heard at a for-profit business. "To serve the needy," you might have heard at a nonprofit. But today, such reasons no longer provide most employees with enough justification to put everything they've got into their work.

While I was leading a workshop about purpose, one CEO participant in the manufacturing business said, "My employees don't care about anything except a paycheck." From that statement alone I made some educated guesses about his people:

- Many are probably living paycheck to paycheck, so of course money is important. It's the *first* reason why they work, but it doesn't have to be the *only* reason.
- If money is truly the only reason they work, the company's leaders have missed the opportunity to provide any other reason to work.
- This CEO either doesn't understand or doesn't know how to express the importance of community.
- That company probably has higher than average turnover.
- Instead of confronting the situation they have created, its leaders probably wonder why "no one in this generation is willing to work hard anymore."

When you boil it down, what do people really want from their work? What general principles hold true from entry level to the CEO? I see four universal desires:

- Compensation that is perceived as fair.
- A sense of community, which includes being recognized as a unique human being and working with others to achieve goals greater than anyone alone could achieve.
- A sense of purpose, which creates a clear understanding of why the work matters. Clarity of purpose speaks to the heart and links the harder aspects of their day-to-day work with a greater good they can feel proud of.
- Challenges and opportunities to learn and grow.

When people get stuck exclusively on the first desire—compensation—they become mercenaries. They're happy to change jobs to get higher pay, and they'll keep job-hopping year after year unless they feel that too many switches are hurting their reputations. On the other hand, when employers are thoughtful about helping people become energized by the purpose and values of the organization, money takes on less significance and employees are more likely to stay.

For instance, if a leader says, "We will have the largest market share in our industry, provide superior return to shareholders, and be recognized as a best place to work"—those are measures, not purpose. There's nothing wrong with having those measures, but they don't mention why market share, ROI, or workplace rankings are worth pursuing. They won't speak to the heart of anyone looking for purpose.

Let's consider another iconic company that has maintained its core purpose over many decades, despite enormous changes in its mission, goals, and business model. About a century ago, Walt Disney's purpose for his company was "to create happiness."[6] His mission might have been described as "using the power of storytelling to entertain, inform, and inspire." The details of how the company would achieve that purpose and how they'd measure their success would change dramatically, as it evolved from a small animation studio to a global entertainment giant.

In a healthy organization, purpose rarely changes, while mission and strategies change from time to time, and goals and tactics change quarterly or annually to adjust to changing conditions.

WHAT MAKES A STRONG PURPOSE?

I've found that the best examples of purpose share five characteristics:

- They're memorable—and usually no more than six words long.
- They're emotive—triggering a feeling in the listener.
- They're inclusive—broad enough that everyone in the organization can relate their work to the purpose.
- They're distinctive—describing how the world is different because this one unique organization exists.
- They're authentic—true to who the organization really is.

When these elements combine into a single compelling purpose, organizations have a significant head start toward employee buy-in. Some examples:

- Nike's vision is: "To bring inspiration and innovation to every athlete in the world."[7]
- Morgan Jewelers is: "Making a difference in families for generations."[8]
- The spatial mapping company Aero-Graphics is: "Bringing our world into view."[9]
- Campbell's Soup is: "Connecting people through food they love."[10]
- The food bank founded by the famous Zingerman's Deli in Ann Arbor, Michigan, has a purpose to "Alleviate hunger and eliminate its causes in our community."[11]

Each of these is inspiring and meets the other criteria as well. The next question to consider is the difference between a leader (or small group of leaders) creating a compelling purpose versus tapping into Collective Genius.

LONE GENIUS VERSUS COLLECTIVE GENIUS

I've found that there are basically two ways to come up with a compelling purpose that includes all the characteristics we've been talking about.

First, you can have a single brilliant visionary leader who already has a crystal-clear purpose. Think of Bill Gates in the late 1970s and early 1980s, telling Microsoft's employees that they were working toward a future with a personal computer on every desk in every home and office, all of them running Microsoft software. That kind of leader is one in a million, so don't feel bad if you aren't up there with Gates, Disney, Walton, or Jobs.

It can be tempting to think that you can impose your vision even if you don't have that kind of one-in-a-million clarity. But if you try, you may end up doing more harm than good—especially if you try to ram your idea down the organization's throat.

The good news is that you don't need to rely on being (or working for) one amazing visionary. Instead, you can tap the Collective Genius of a broad cross section of employees, leading to some amazing input and widespread buy-in. And you don't need a Fortune 500 budget to do it. Let's consider the case study of one client that nailed its purpose through the Collective Genius Process.

Alta Equipment Group has deep roots as a family-owned, second-generation company. Under CEO Ryan Greenawalt, they identified a model to successfully acquire similar businesses, went public to fund that business model, and built a multibillion-dollar business in just a few years. Each acquired business, though in the same line of work, had a different purpose and mission, and some had none at all. They all lacked a common, compelling purpose and a common language for describing why their work was important and why employees should care.

Sensing that there would be great benefit to bringing together the leaders of his different businesses to create a common vision, Greenawalt asked us to guide his team through alignment around one compelling vision. The process is one you can also apply, no matter the size of your company. We led Alta's 40 key leaders through a sequence of four main steps to create, test, and roll out a compelling, unified purpose to team members across the company.

First, we shared the five criteria of a compelling purpose listed earlier in this chapter with each leader ahead of our in-person session.

Second, the team gathered and formed small groups so team members could compare ideas and stimulate their thinking by hearing other ideas.

Third, each team shared their best thinking, which was written on old-fashioned flip charts so everyone could see it. Then, without any dis-cussion, we asked team members to vote on the ideas they thought were most appealing.

Finally, we solicited volunteers to join a cross-functional committee to wordsmith the most popular concept, test it out with their employees, and report back.

This last step of testing a purpose with employees is very important in generating buy-in. Sometimes we talk with leaders who want to explain their purpose statement or values, and then ask employees, "What do you think?" This approach is usually well intended, but it ignores the fact that the final statement of purpose or values won't be accompanied by an expla-nation. It will have to stand on its own. So, to get a true sense of how peo-ple experience such statements, it's important to share the actual wording without explanation, then ask questions like "What does this mean to you?" or "Do you see yourself in this purpose?" This is the difference between deep listening about an idea versus merely 'splaining it!

At Alta, the result of our idea generation and road-testing process was the purpose of "Delivering Trust That Makes a Difference." This became more than a nice-sounding phrase; it became an actionable guide to help everyone at Alta set priorities and make decisions in line with purpose. People at Alta frequently ask, "What solution will get us closer to our pur-pose?" They share the purpose with investors, vendors, customers, and new employees to explain the company's story. It has become an important part of many significant conversations.

MAKING THE CASE FOR VALUES

The same process of tapping into Collective Genius to define an organiza-tion's purpose can also be used to uncover, simplify, and codify its values. Please note that I didn't say "generate" values because they already exist in every organization, whether you're aware of them or not.

We define values as the mutually agreed-upon rules by which peo-ple treat each other and make decisions. Values are also a description of the qualities by which an organization will execute its mission. They are the (often) unwritten agreement among an organization on what kind of behavior is valued and acceptable. As noted in the chapter about simplifying priorities, having more than three or four values dilutes them, because few will remember them all—let alone apply them.

When we interview executives for the first time, we always ask what values they observe in practice in their organization, and the answers are often surprising in their differences. Not only do we hear differences among executives, but we also hear differences from the posters hanging in the break room! Try this exercise yourself: without any advance notice or group discussion, ask your team to write down the values they see being practiced. Then compare notes. There's a good chance the values described will diverge—maybe with variations on the same basic values, but maybe all over the map. In the absence of clearly articulated, often repeated values across an organization, values will often vary by work group, which causes unnecessary confusion, conflict, and misaligned silos. In contrast, organizations that reference and practice their values regularly find that people understand what behaviors are and aren't okay, which helps create a safe space.

The goal is alignment on the most important values as they are actually practiced in the organization, not what you might wish for in a more perfect world. This is why one-word, overly broad values can be meaningless or counterproductive. For instance, "honesty" sounds like an admirable value, but what is the behavior that would demonstrate honesty? How would you know it when you saw it? If you want honesty as a value, add a short description of what specifically you mean by honesty and what that behavior looks like.

IDENTIFYING AND CLARIFYING YOUR VALUES

While the top executives at an organization may have more experience, it's impossible for them to understand how values are practiced throughout an organization. Therefore, tap into the Collective Genius and recruit a small, cross-functional, multi-level, diverse team of five to seven people.

"Cross-functional" should include people not just from different departments but also, if applicable, from different locations. "Multi-level" means giving equal voices to people at different levels of the org chart; the team leaders should be whoever can best manage this process. "Diverse" means people with different backgrounds, time with the company, and experiences.

This team first organizes a survey to a broad group of employees, the more the better, asking key questions, such as:

- How do you generally experience your colleagues' values?
- What behaviors do you believe are treated as okay or not okay?
- What values do you repeatedly see being rewarded?
- When thinking about how to solve a work problem, what values do you consider beyond the impact on our revenue or costs?

The team should analyze the responses for similarities and patterns, then rank the most commonly discussed values and craft language about them for the top three or four to begin identifying and clarifying the organization's values.

Here's an example of how this Collective Genius Process went when working with one of our clients in Kansas City. The values team saw "transparent communication" as a top-five value in the survey responses. Then they created qualifiers to refine it:

- Practice authentic, honest, and open communication.
- Seek to understand others' points of view.
- Gain clear agreement from others before assuming your request is their commitment.

The team tested this value and qualifiers, along with the other top values, asking a sample of team members: "Does this feel true to who we are and the behaviors we value?"

For testing values statements, you might ask, "What behaviors would you expect to see (or not see) if we adopted these values?"

When they finished the process, the organization went from ten values that had been posted on the walls but were generally ignored, to just four values that were easy to understand and remember, each with its own supporting statements:

- *Transparency in All Communications*
- *Act with Integrity*

- *Work Hard and Have Fun*
- *Team of Professionals*

We regularly ask our clients how often they hear values referenced by their teams when setting strategy, priorities, and making decisions. In a healthy culture with widespread buy-in, the discussion becomes more thorough. In addition to financial considerations, compelling purpose and values also inform the options and outcome.

Five Tips to Clarify and Apply Your Values

1. Are these values that represent how we hire, recognize, and reward people?
2. Are these values one or two words and easily remembered?
3. Do we have four or fewer values?
4. Are these values referenced in decision-making on a regular basis?
5. Are they used as a behavior benchmark in performance reviews?

APPLYING PURPOSE AND VALUES TO EVERYDAY ACTIVITIES

Healthy organizations have learned how to use purpose and values to generate buy-in while driving game-changing results. Let's examine four situations in which purpose and values become valuable tools: hiring, decision-making, feedback, and prioritization.

Because of the importance of purpose for today's talent pool, organizations that have gone through the effort to create a compelling purpose have a leg up in hiring. The job interview is an opportunity to share the company's purpose with the applicant and ask a key question: "Please take a minute to consider how you see yourself in our purpose. What does it mean to you?" Listen carefully to the response and watch their expressions as they answer. If you generally hire for skills but the applicant does not connect with your purpose, you should probably keep looking. You don't want to hire someone who will leave as soon as they find an organization that needs their skills and more closely aligns with their purpose.

Likewise, when interviewing, bring up the company's values with the applicant. Ask if they can relate to and believe in those values. Then ask, "Can you think of a time when the value of X was violated where you worked? What happened and how did you handle it?" You will learn a lot about whether this applicant will fit into your culture and get a gauge on how likely they are to be a long-term team player.

A second opportunity to leverage purpose is in decision-making. Every team we've worked with comes up with lots of different solutions for consideration when solving an issue. One criterion by which to evaluate them is by asking, "Which one is most closely aligned with, or gets us closest to, accomplishing our purpose and is most aligned with our values?" This especially applies to non-obvious areas such as which vendor to choose. If a vendor selection is made only on the best price but there's misalignment on values, the team is setting themselves up for predictable challenges down the road.

This method to make decisions keeps your purpose and values front and center while modeling how to use them.

Values and purpose are also reference points when providing feedback that makes a difference. Sometimes well-intentioned leaders will tell a team member, "Good job!" without referring to any specific action. This is worse than not saying anything for the confusion it causes. *Which of the 30 things I've done today is she referring to? Does she really know what I do? Does she tell everyone the same "Good job"?* Instead, try connecting a specific behavior you observe to a value. It might sound like this: "When you openly shared with the team yesterday what you could not get done on time, it really demonstrated our value of transparent communications. Thank you for setting that example."

Finally, purpose is useful when ranking priorities. When we are with teams, we usually ask, "How many of you have more things on your to-do list than you have time in the day?" and 100% of the hands go up!

A similar question of "Which of these options will allow us to achieve our purpose more quickly?" helps people select what's most important to get done first.

Ideas Worth Considering

1. What are our opportunities to reinforce the use of purpose and values in everyday conversations?
2. How well does our compelling purpose stack up against the criteria mentioned in this chapter? Are there ways we could use it more effectively in recruiting, decision-making, and providing feedback?
3. How explicit are our values? Do we describe what behavior you might see when the value is in action? Do we cascade these in decision-making processes, hiring/firing, feedback, and recognition?

Part 3

SEIZING OPPORTUNITIES TO REINFORCE BUY-IN

After you've built a buy-in culture, you've got to stay vigilant to maintain it. Otherwise, the culture will slowly fade, like taillights disappearing in the distance. Things will go off the rails as your best talent drifts away, hiring great people becomes harder, productivity drops, and a sense of malaise sets in.

Every organization goes through cycles when the biggest challenges shift. Sometimes, what feels most pressing is industry or market disruptions from outside the organization. Other times, the biggest challenges emerge from trouble within the organization. The chapters in part 3 address the common pain points your company might be experiencing right now.

Even the best organizations will experience most of these pain points at one time or another, so reading all of these chapters in order will help you prepare for that potential future. But you may prefer to skip directly to the chapter that aligns most closely with your current pain points. If so, you can choose just one of these "Four A" strategies to begin making immediate improvements to your specific situation.

If You Are Experiencing:	Start Here:
• Urgent threats to your business, such as a major new competitor. • Slowly evolving malaise or performance issues that may eventually rise to a crisis level.	Chapter 11: "Adapt When a Crisis or Kudzu Throws You Off Track"
• Turnover rates that have been creeping upward. • Difficulty in hiring new people. • Difficulty in retaining good people. • Complaints that performance reviews are ineffective. • Complaints that written job descriptions don't match people's actual jobs.	Chapter 12: "Accelerate Buy-In During Recruiting, Job Interviews, and Performance Reviews"
• General malaise among the team. • Failure to celebrate wins, which makes people feel like their hard work isn't appreciated. • Frustration that the team isn't giving it their all to create extraordinary results. • Messages from the top are mostly ignored or quickly forgotten, rather than internalized.	Chapter 13: "Adopt Modeling, Cascading, and Celebrating to Reinvigorate Buy-In"
• Strategic planning that lacks buy-in and mostly sits on the shelf gathering dust. • Missed deadlines and projects not getting completed. • Lack of accountability for key tasks needed to execute strategy. • Too many competing priorities.	Chapter 14: "Apply Collective Genius to Strategic Planning"

Chapter 11 addresses the occasional crises that every organization faces, along with slow-growing problems I call kudzu. In these situations, a leader's natural response might be to take charge and make decisions. But we'll show how it's far better for changing behaviors to get "all hands on deck" to address the real issue, come up with solutions, and implement them with greater buy-in.

Chapter 12 considers new ways to think about hiring and two-way performance conversations to engage, motivate, and increase buy-in. We'll explore powerful techniques to retain talent—without relying primarily on money.

Chapter 13 turns to three powerful leadership practices—modeling, cascading, and celebrating—that can improve performance immediately while growing the long-term capabilities of your people.

Finally, chapter 14 applies the Collective Genius Process to the all-important process of strategic planning. It shows why the typical approach to strategic planning tends to go off the rails during execution, and how to hit your goals more often by helping people actually care about and execute your quarterly or annual plans.

Chapter 11

ADAPT WHEN A CRISIS OR KUDZU THROWS YOU OFF TRACK

There's an old joke about a CEO being abruptly fired and seeing his replacement in the hallway as he's leaving. "Is there anything you want to tell me?" asks the incoming CEO. "Yes!" the former CEO replies. "Everything you need to know is located in three envelopes in the top desk drawer in your office. Open just one at a time when things go off track."

Sure enough, a few months later, things start going wrong. The CEO remembers the envelopes and opens the first one, which says simply: "Blame prior management." He does so and gets through the problem. Six months after that, another big problem arises. The second envelope contains one word: "Reorganize." So he does, and things improve again.

The following year, yet another crisis happens, the biggest one yet. The CEO opens the third envelope and sees his predecessor's final advice: "Prepare three envelopes!"

Leaders usually laugh at this joke with grim recognition. All organizations go off the rails sometimes, whether suddenly during a crisis or slowly as "kudzu" grows around them and begins to choke the life out of them. In my experience as a CEO, such problems sometimes happen due to a totally external, unexpected event or force. Other times they happen because the team has collectively taken their eye off the ball. Either way, it was deeply frustrating to work with my team on carefully crafted plans that no longer made sense. But as I gained experience, I began to accept that problems would be inevitable no matter what I did. Identifying the reasons was less important than preventing temporary setbacks from escalating into bigger problems.

I didn't have the power to prevent market forces from throwing us off track—but I *did* have the power to choose my responses wisely. As the joke notes, the most common responses to both crises and kudzu are blaming some outside force or prior management, or doing a major reorganization (with layoffs usually included). But there's a better way to respond (and increase the odds you'll achieve the results you want), as you'll see in this chapter. The fastest and most impactful recoveries involve concepts we introduced earlier: tapping into the Collective Genius of the team, engaging others in ranking possible solutions, overcommunicating to foster buy-in, monitoring changes, and adjusting the plan as required. These processes don't take much time and are fundamental building blocks of creating the Buy-In Advantage.

THE DIFFERENCE BETWEEN CRISES AND KUDZU

You've heard the military expression "No plan survives the first contact with war." And so it is with business. No matter how well we prepare, eventually the stuff hits the fan—hopefully not hard enough to destroy the entire business. Here are just a few examples of unexpected crises I've been forced to deal with as a leader:

- Server hacks that brought down all of my company's online operations.
- The 9/11 terrorist attacks, which killed 13 members of my team.
- Two global health epidemics.
- Cancellation of a multimillion-dollar line of credit, despite exceeding every requirement of our lender.

- An SEC investigation prompted by the plaintiff's lawyer for a disgruntled former employee.
- A competitor stealing lines of code and poaching customers with it.

Hopefully you will go through nothing like these dramatic moments in your business journey. What makes them especially hard is that an initial crisis often leads to secondary effects that linger long after. For example, during the global financial crisis of 2008–2009, my company's bank pulled a $30 million line of credit. We had only a couple of million drawn down and were in full compliance with all the covenants. However, at the time, federal regulators were crushing the banks with stress tests that caused them to pull back on credit. We took the hit and were forced to quickly find operating cash from other places, while cutting expenses to the bone. This secondary effect lingered for many months after.

But as bad as crises can be, they have at least one major upside. Crises announce themselves in a dramatic way, and everyone can see what's going wrong in real time, or close to it. That's in contrast to the slow-growing, harder-to-detect, but often even more damaging process I call kudzu, after the leafy Asian vine that became a menace across the southern United States. The US government introduced it in the South during the Great Depression, to choke off weeds. Unfortunately, the experiment worked so well that kudzu—which can sometimes grow as rapidly as a foot per day— has been out of control for decades and chokes off much more desirable plants.

Similarly, business kudzu is a slow malaise that sneaks up on you at first, until it strangles the life from your culture, your people, and your company's results. Gradually, bit by bit, the leadership's focus changes and the disciplined execution of objectives becomes lax. Implicit assumptions replace clear communication, which allows each executive to operate in their own sphere of responsibility, based on a different view of what's true.

There are eight symptoms we referenced back in chapter 3 that are typical of organizations whose results are choked by kudzu:

1. Wages are increasing but key talent leaves anyway.
2. Meetings start late, are canceled at the last minute, or run over.
3. Key objectives or measures are frequently missed.

4. People do exactly what they are asked (but no more!).
5. Engagement scores are low or are in decline.
6. People aren't clear on how the organization is making a difference.
7. People are unaware or in conflict about who is doing what.
8. Key customers are leaving or reducing service.

This malaise may start as a slow creep, with only one or two of these symptoms. But once the kudzu gets established, it can start growing and spreading quickly. So you need to be on the lookout for kudzu and diagnose it right away, if you want the best shot at defeating it.

Doing such a diagnosis will be easier or harder depending on the level of trust among the executive team. And that's tricky because in low-trust organizations, the politically skilled can masquerade as team players when in fact they are entirely self-serving. One clear symptom of a low-trust team is that you won't hear any unpopular opinions expressed. If you have any inkling that the leadership team is low trust, it probably is—which means defeating the kudzu will be even trickier.

BEWARE THE FOG OF WAR DURING A CRISIS

In the 2003 documentary *The Fog of War*, Robert McNamara opens up about the highs and lows of his famous career, which included stints as president of the Ford Motor Company and as US secretary of defense during the Vietnam War. His biggest insight is that during a crisis such as a war, it's very hard to get an accurate read on how things are really going. The "fog" of ambiguity and confusion often leads to two big mistakes that prevent leaders from understanding and aligning on what needs to be done to improve the situation.

The first mistake originates when a leader who is known for being smart and decisive rushes to "do something" during a crisis. Decisiveness is a great quality most of the time, but in times of crisis it often causes mistakes. Here's why: if you rely on your personal experience and analysis alone to take action quickly, you might make things worse because the current situation doesn't fit the norms of your past experience. It's more important than ever to solicit a wide range of possible solutions and trust the Collective Genius Process.

Back when I did pilot training for multi-engine jets, I was cautioned that when you lose an engine the first thing you should do is say, "Oh, shit!" to slow yourself down from accidentally shutting down the remaining good engine. That expletive gives you a second to catch your breath and think before acting. The same is true in business—and you can afford to take more than a second before reacting.

The second common mistake is becoming overly obsessed by the crisis at the expense of the rest of your business. The crisis needs to be kept in perspective. Again from my aviation training, I learned about Eastern Airlines Flight 401, which crashed into the Florida Everglades in 1972, killing 101 people. The problem started with a landing gear indicator failure on the approach to land in Miami, which should *not* have been fatal even if it couldn't be fixed in the air. Tragically, however, every member of the cockpit crew became so absorbed in addressing the potential landing gear issue that no one noticed that the autopilot had accidentally kicked off. In the overcast night, they didn't notice a gradual descent into the Everglades swamp. If only one of the four cockpit members had been assigned to focus solely on flying the plane while the other three worked on the landing gear crisis, the disaster could probably have been avoided.

A PROCESS FOR ADDRESSING KUDZU OR A CRISIS

Here's a simple four-step plan if you are feeling under pressure to make things happen and don't want to make mistakes. First is to gather and evaluate all the evidence. The important part of this step is to separate what is factual from the meaning we assign to the facts. Second is prioritizing the most important issue to be addressed since tackling them all at once causes confusion and suboptimal results. Next is generating criteria and aligning on what "great" will look like in a solution. Finally, the fourth step is to brainstorm and then select a plan including owners, assumptions, and timetables.

Evaluating the Facts of a Crisis

One of the skills of highly effective leadership teams is the ability to separate indisputable facts from debatable opinions or beliefs. When you hear an observation about the situation, ask yourself, "Is this something a totally objective robot observer would perceive, or is this an *interpretation* of the facts?"

Whenever I explain this concept to a room of leaders, I like to show a slide with a picture of an American stop sign. "What do you see?" I ask simply.

"Duh, it's a stop sign," is a predictable response. Then I ask, "What would a totally objective and ignorant robot see?" Suddenly, the answers change. Now it's described as a piece of metal with eight sides, or a red sign with white letters that spell STOP. Then we go further to consider that the robot might not know what S-T-O-P means. Everything we believe about the image is really an interpretation, based on our specific knowledge of colors, shapes, letters, and driving in the United States.

Returning to McNamara's insights in *The Fog of War*: he stresses that it's essential to gather hard data and challenge what you *think* you plainly see during a crisis. Sometimes what we "see" is distorted by what we believe, not what is actually happening. That was true during the Vietnam War, when McNamara's Pentagon focused on the wrong metrics (such as relative body counts) in evaluating how the US military was doing and whether the war was winnable.

So an important analysis—especially when under pressure—is to ask, "Are we looking at the data itself or the meaning we're subconsciously assigning to the data?" Making decisions based on interpretations without identifying them as such can lead to poor choices. This is not to imply that meaning is unimportant. We'll see how to assign and apply meanings when we take the next step in creating solutions. But it's time to prioritize the evidence of the situation to identify what's causing the most pain or throwing results off track that is *under our control*. No sense complaining about "the economy" or "competitors" or "the weather."

What Do We Wish We Had Known or Done Back Then?

In working with clients, one of the most important exercises we've found to prevent future kudzu is to look back in hindsight and identify whatever factors contributed to that situation. There are several key questions to this analysis:

1. Are there activity measures in place that could have predicted the current situation, if we hadn't overlooked them?
2. Are there processes in place that could have lessened or prevented the situation? If so, do we have evidence they were faithfully followed?
3. Are there activity measures or processes that we *don't* have that we should now create in order to prevent a recurrence or give us more warning that something bad is about to happen?

Please note that these questions do not refer to KPIs or standard performance metrics. Those are usually backward-facing ways to evaluate the normal course of business, when what we need are early warnings of extraordinary problems. For example, this month's profit and operating margin are the result of decisions made months earlier, and don't allow us to predict what will happen next.

In contrast, activity measures are easily identified, and spotting trends in them can allow us to predict problems in advance. A simple example is that revenue is the result and the preceding activity might be the number of weekly sales calls or inbound inquiries. Knowing the trends in sales calls or inbounds is a better predictor of the future than this month's revenue.

New measures should provide an early warning system as to the accuracy of the assumptions and the health of the business. For example, if factory output has declined due to a lack of materials, a new measure might be the number of weeks of supply on hand for each manufacturing component.

Prioritizing the Problems to Be Solved First

In the example I gave earlier in which the bank pulled our credit line, my executive team could have immediately launched a search for another bank. But that would take time, and first we had a much more urgent need to find a source of short-term cash to tide us over. So prioritizing our problems was the first step before we could start pursuing solutions.

You will need a disciplined approach to prevent your team from racing headfirst into devising and executing solutions. That's a dangerous trap that can make things worse. First you need to collectively analyze all the problems in front of you. Then go through each problem in sequence until you have consensus on the top two or three that require immediate focus. Only then, after identifying and prioritizing the key issues, is it time to start creating solutions. That's what the crew of that Florida flight might have done differently to avoid getting overwhelmed by the landing gear glitch.

To take a more recent example, when the initial wave of Covid disruptions rolled through the United States in the spring of 2020, several of my clients were alarmed about the impact on their businesses—and justifiably so! Although I didn't have the answers or the ability to predict how things would unfold, I advised them to take a deep breath and look hard at what had just changed, both internally and externally. Next was to separate the facts from their instinctive interpretation—the meaning they attached to those facts. Clearly identifying their *assumptions* about the future would help align their teams' Collective Genius so they could brainstorm creative solutions.

Here are three questions you can ask your team about their assumptions:

- Based on our analysis, what do we believe to be true about the future?
- What would be the markers to indicate whether our assumption is true or not true?
- Who on the team will monitor those markers, how frequently, and how often will we do team check-ins about them?

Record these assumptions because you will be referring to them regularly in the future to see if new data warrants revisiting them!

What Criteria Will Define a Great Solution?

As we learned in chapter 5, the best way to solve a problem is to be explicit about the criteria that need to be met in defining a great solution. Ask the room exactly what you're trying to accomplish first. Remember the example of needing to nail down short-term survival financing before seeking a new long-term bank.

Often, we observe leaders agreeing on a plan without agreeing on which measures the team hopes to see changed and by how much. Your explicit criteria should clearly indicate what results are expected and when. This forecasting is important whether you're trying to address a crisis or kudzu. Defining a forecast goal helps everyone optimize their proposed solutions. And it's important that these forecasts result from a team discussion, not a spreadsheet exercise handed down from the finance department. The former creates alignment and commitment while the latter ("We need to cut costs by 10%") is simply a check-the-box exercise that can hinder buy-in.

After the team has aligned on criteria for a great solution, it's time for individual brainstorming on your own about the highest priority problem. Then you can reassemble your team for the presentation of their ideas.

Discussing, Debating, and Deciding

Ask your team to share their proposed solutions one at a time, and *do not engage in any discussion about them yet*. Discussion at this point is counterproductive and will hinder open sharing of ideas. Just summarize them on a whiteboard or via a similar method.

The reason not to discuss ideas is simply that team time is too valuable to spend on ideas that don't have the attention and interest of the whole team. Too often we observe teams spending time debating the first idea mentioned and then complain they run out of time when they get to a real "meaty" discussion.

Once everyone has spoken, ask the room if any of the solutions are similar enough to be combined. If so, consolidate the options on the whiteboard.

Then ask everyone in the room to vote, using the "weigh the ox" process we discussed in chapter 4. Again, no discussion is necessary at this point. You don't want to trigger groupthink by tipping your hand about which ideas you like best.

Hopefully, one idea will emerge as the best-fitting criterion. You can then ask for two volunteers to expand the solution concept and create a more complete plan for the team to review and comment on. If two ideas are neck and neck in the voting, you can do this step for both ideas.

Make sure these expanded plans answer a key question: "What will we deprioritize or stop doing to create the capacity to execute this plan?" Too many times, great solutions fail because they get added to a laundry list of other priorities. As noted above, you can't ignore the importance of continuing to run the business well while dealing with the crisis. Revisiting your top strategic priorities and eliminating or delaying other priorities to make space will increase the odds of successful execution.

When the detailed plan or plans are presented, it's finally time for a full discussion to vet them, explore any possible drawbacks, and (if necessary) vote again on the two finalists.

Chunking the Work!

Great ideas that will really move the needle can seem daunting. Where will we find time to do it? How could we get all this done? Who has the capacity to make it happen? To keep this feeling from causing people to delay implementation, it's important to "chunk" the work. Break it down into smaller pieces that can be accomplished and celebrated. The sense of accomplishment will propel the team to take on the next chunk!

Then you can proceed to communicate to engage (see below) and implement the solution to the highest-priority problem. Then the team can go through a similar process to address the second and third biggest problems, if necessary.

Overcommunicate to Engage

When things are going off track, everybody knows. People are naturally on high alert and if nothing is offered for context, they will make up stories. That's just human nature. Imagine the power of harnessing all the energy that goes into fear and gossip!

At times like these, lean toward overcommunicating more than you might think necessary. Messages should be frequent and use a variety of modes of communication (break room, social media, chat rooms, Zoom or Teams, one-on-ones, and so on). They should remind people of the context, be factually (even brutally) honest, and provide a sense of hope. The latter is especially important. People will feel hope if the leader's messages seem honest, authentic, and grounded in a realistic plan to make things better. Please note that you have to be specific—a vague message of "We've got this, no need to panic, just trust me!" will come across as tone deaf. If you don't get specific, you may damage the group's confidence instead of lifting it.

Please also keep in mind that your messages should be simple enough for anyone to understand and remember. If you can reference back to actions or events that people are already familiar with, and if you can make most of your points through stories, your words will be most effective.

A best practice is to set a messaging goal for each of your leaders and ask them to set expectations about re-messaging from leader to leader, department to department, to reinforce a consistent set of talking points.

Monitoring Assumptions and Results

After you have assembled the evidence, prioritized the issues to be addressed, and developed criteria, let's go to the final piece in the four-step process. It's great to think you're finished when the plan is made, but it's actually just creating a road map for what the future will look like. The team should be explicit about ownership of:

- Measures: Who owns monitoring and reporting on these progress indicators?
- Processes: Who will create new ones or modify existing ones?
- Objectives: Who will drive their accomplishment?

It's also worth having an explicit discussion about when reporting will occur, both in formal meetings and via unscheduled updates. For example, if the team decides that an assumption about interest rates is a key part of the path forward, what are the standing instructions to the person monitoring interest rates to report back between meetings?

A great unknown during the pandemic was how long it would last and how severe it would be. One of our clients, Destination Homes, saw a dramatic decrease in home sales. The leaders knew they had to cut costs, which meant slowing or stopping the building of new homes. But how much to cut back was a huge unknown! If the cutback was too severe, there would not be enough homes to sell when demand returned. But if it was not deep enough, carrying costs would severely drain cash while they sat on unsold inventory financed by bank loans.

The executive team came together and developed a list of key assumptions about the future. These assumptions informed their most likely market scenario, which informed their plan. We knew that most of the assumptions would be wrong; we just didn't know which ones, by how much, and when!

For the top two or three assumptions, one person was asked to monitor it and report back if the data varied from the assumption in the future. This allowed the Destination team to have a dynamic plan to respond to the market as they learned about variances from their assumptions!

This practice of monitoring ongoing situations is a regular part of the intelligence process in the military. They monitor movement of troops, equipment, satellite and missile launches, and construction activities as well as government and leader activities in order to predict what will happen next. These predictions give the military more time to react when things change in ways they do not anticipate. It's a good practice that should be used much more widely in the business world.

Another aspect of monitoring involves what is happening within the organization. This includes making sure that assumptions, measures, process, and objectives monitoring that were created to address the situation have a place for review in standing meetings. Especially if it's kudzu, the solutions will be iterative, meaning that whatever you came up with will need to be adjusted as new information or results become available. And if the crisis was caused by kudzu, the changes that are implemented need to take hold faster than new kudzu can grow!

Standing meetings are a great opportunity to ask yourselves:

- Is this plan playing out as we expected?
- If not, have we communicated it fully to our teams?
- Do they have the necessary tools and training to make it happen?
- Has it been appropriately prioritized?

If you've done everything you can to make it successful and been patient enough to see the results you forecast, then it's time to repeat the cycle from the top and adjust the plan!

In summary, the three steps are gaining alignment on what's happening; using Collective Genius to create solutions including measures, processes, and objectives; and monitoring assumptions and results. They work in both crises and in strangulation by kudzu. Then, as in ordinary times, overcommunicating the context, the plan, and everyone's expected contributions can be one of the most impactful ways leaders can change the direction of the organization.

GOING EVEN FURTHER WITH COLLECTIVE GENIUS

If time permits, there is a more broad-based approach that results in even better thinking: ask all employees for suggestions in solving the crisis.

This approach changed the culture and company results forever at CHG Healthcare. Leadership at this medical staffing company projected they would lose about a third of their revenue during the great financial crisis. People are their number one expense. Therefore, it was obvious that a significant layoff was required. Most companies would have the executive team meet privately and decide who should be let go. But CHG chose a different path, which impacted their results and culture for years to follow.[1]

The executive team leveled with every member of the company, explaining the need for dramatic expense cuts and asking for ideas from every single person about what could be done other than laying people off. They received thousands of suggestions, which a committee evaluated and prioritized. For example, the company adopted strict new travel expense policies, as suggested by frontline travelers. This process prevented a draconian layoff and cemented their belief in "putting people first."

This process took longer and was more complex than just having a few executives make decisions in private, but also yielded other benefits. The inclusive listening drove a spike in buy-in. CHG subsequently became more profitable than competitors because of turnover of only about half the industry average. This reduced turnover meant less time and effort were spent on recruiting and training as well as less stress created by vacant positions. Those millions not spent dropped to their bottom line and gave them more flexibility and capability in a very tough business.

The CHG story is a vivid reminder that the people who know best what's going on are the people doing the work. And they also know how best to address challenges.

Whether it's kudzu or a crisis causing results to go off track, separating story from fact and using Collective Genius to create thoughtful responses are powerful tools to create buy-in. Next, we consider how to leverage everyday activities when things are on track to supercharge results!

Ideas Worth Considering

1. How effective is our team in generating what's-working/what's-not lists, selecting one issue to address, and setting criteria for what great looks like?
2. After we make a decision, what process do we use to identify what measures we will monitor, who will own it, and the rhythm of checking in on progress?
3. Are there opportunities where we can better "chunk" our work to make it more digestible and provide more opportunities for celebration?

Chapter 12

ACCELERATE BUY-IN DURING RECRUITING, JOB INTERVIEWS, AND PERFORMANCE REVIEWS

Many years ago, I was a passenger on a flight where I witnessed firsthand my first (and hopefully only!) attempted airplane hijacking. I remember it vividly and, believe it or not, it continues to inform my thinking about the interview process and buy-in. Yes, I was on the receiving end of an interview question from a hijacker!

It was the last of three long Delta Air Lines flights heading back to South Carolina from a salmon fishing trip with buddies in Alaska. The first two red-eyes had left me quite tired, so I stretched out on a bench in the Atlanta airport, trying to catch a nap before my final connection. I awoke to hear a man yelling into a nearby pay phone: "I know I owe you the money! I'll get you the money!" He was quite agitated. After a few minutes, I went back to trying to nap and thought nothing more of it.

We boarded the jet, and I was fortunate to nab a first-class window seat. Again I fell into a slumber, only to be awakened near the end of the flight by that same voice. This time the guy was running up and down the aisles yelling, "Stand up if you believe in Jesus Christ! We are going to crash, but we will all be saved!" As you can imagine, I was utterly shocked and confused. I watched him run to the front of the plane, right near my seat, and lunge toward the emergency exit as if to open it. A flight attendant restrained him, but the man grabbed her and pushed her hard against the cockpit door, demanding to be let inside.

Amazingly, she pretended to be unflustered, using her best school-teacher voice to try to calm this crazy man down. "Sir, we are about to land. You have to take a seat and put on a seat belt." She pointed him to the empty aisle seat next to me. Even more amazingly, he sat down, put on his seat belt, and stuck out his hand to me, as if nothing strange had just happened. Then he calmly asked me the interview question: "Are you union?" I didn't know what to say and mumbled a noncommittal response. He went on to explain that he could get me a good union job. He was suddenly in a conversational mode, as if we had just struck up a normal airplane seat-mate chat. The plane landed shortly thereafter, and federal agents stormed onboard to arrest him for assaulting a flight attendant. The incident made national news.[1]

What does any of this have to do with employee buy-in? I later realized that as crazy as this man obviously was, his question about being in a union was an attempt to establish a personal connection. He was trying to identify if I was like him.

Buy-in isn't the result of occasional town hall meetings or all-staff emails; it has to be baked into everyday moments. This chapter offers nontraditional approaches to routine events such as interviewing, hiring, performance feedback, and connecting with every member of your team—from their first interaction with the company through their day-to-day work. We'll explore some best practices in these less dramatic, everyday situations.

You might think these goals would already be a huge priority for all leaders, but they aren't always obvious. Consider Jeff Schneiter, who was the general manager of a successful Cadillac dealership in Salt Lake City, Utah. He was under pressure to significantly cut costs and increase profits. He told me he had already reduced expenses "to the bone" and asked what was left to be done.

We talked about reducing turnover, which he had not yet considered as a strategy to improve profits. He did some checking and found that the dealership's turnover rate was about 50%! Unfortunately for Jeff, Salt Lake City had one of the lowest unemployment rates in the country at the time, resulting in bidding wars for great employees with experience as well as entry-level employees. But Jeff then devoted an entire year to applying buy-in strategies to the dealership's everyday activities, like holding Discovery Sessions to learn about the experience of the frontline people and what they thought would improve it. As a result, he was able to drastically reduce turnover and increase profits—with no additional cash outlay! His savings came from costs that are not obvious to see on the profit statement.

The Hidden Costs of Turnover

One unfortunate miss in traditional financial reporting is a lack of transparency on the costs of turnover. These costs include sourcing candidates, evaluating resumes, scheduling interviews, interviewing, hiring, and training. And that doesn't even include the loss of productivity when the position is vacant. Unfortunately, these costs are hidden within the profit and loss statement under general accounts like payroll. Gallup estimates that the cost of turnover is between half and two times a position's salary[2] Yet there is compelling research that can help inform how we break this cycle. McKinsey reports when employees line up with company values, they have stronger engagement and heightened loyalty, which translates directly to lower turnover.[3]

Here's a warning before we dive in: it takes more time to do all these things differently, with a focus on buy-in—but the payoff will be huge! There is an opportunity to bake Buy-In Advantage techniques into every key people process. The payoff is an improvement in profitability because less time will be focused on hiring and retraining (which takes away from everyone's day jobs) and more will be spent on gaining expertise. When I asked Jeff about the benefits of applying the techniques above and beyond profit, he told me his people had more experience and could apply it to do an even better job.

GET THE BEST TALENT AND KEEP THEM BOUGHT IN!

Let's start with recruiting, interviewing, and hiring processes. When the typical company needs to fill a role, it posts a job description, a salary range, and a hiring manager. Someone in HR writes up a recruitment ad and places it on various job sites. Then HR waits for incoming resumes and evaluates them to decide who to interview. There's usually a falloff between interviews scheduled and those who actually show up. The selection is made from among those who interview better than others, assuming the job offer is accepted.

Recruiting new talent often focuses on salary and job descriptions, which is what most leaders were trained to do. Unfortunately, that "conventional wisdom" can lead new hires to start feeling disengaged even before day one. Instead, a better hiring process will generate talent pools of the right kinds of people and foster immediate buy-in by focusing on the organization's compelling purpose and values. Adding in the practice of behavioral-based interviewing will further increase immediate buy-in and long-term employee retention. In this section we'll also consider messaging to potential candidates and using the interview process to predict future performance.

The first and often overlooked step in hiring is to determine exactly the type of person you want to hire. Usually this is defined as years of experience doing certain tasks or a specialized degree or training certificate. These are table stakes and fine to keep. But organizations committed to a culture of buy-in take the additional step of identifying the characteristics and culture fit of the people they need. These characteristics are identified by answering the questions "Are they one of us?" and "Do they have skills that complement those we already have on the team?"

The first question of "one of us" is important if the objective is to reduce turnover. Over half of Gen Z workers say they have a best friend at work.[4] So an important recruitment strategy is to get new people to join your team who will bond with those already on the team. Sometimes this process is easy. If you are a gym, you are likely to attract people interested in and committed to fitness. But what if you are a paper company, logistics company, or staffing company? Look at your purpose! If the purpose meets the criteria we explored in chapter 10, and if your day-to-day culture fully supports that purpose, then finding others like you will become much easier.

Consider Dutch Bros Coffee, a western US chain of very modest drive-through coffee shops. They provide free clothing each month to their hourly associates. Not just any clothing—everything bears the Dutch Bros logo and is practical for everyday use. It might be jackets one month, pullovers the next, light shirts, and so on.[5] This giveaway is powerful in generating retention for a number of reasons:

- Clothing is a major expense for many hourly employees. Dutch Bros provides it free and encourages them to wear it outside of work, which has the added benefit of great advertising!
- They have no dress code for associates except that they need to wear at least one item with a visible logo. Unlike McDonald's and many other customer-facing employers with strict dress codes, this allows freedom of expression for every associate.
- The logoed clothing creates a sense of community among the associates, signaling "I am one of us." It's a clever way to reinforce the sense of community at relatively low cost.

Please note that this concept of "one of us" has nothing to do with race, ethnicity, gender, religion, or political beliefs. In healthy organizations it's an attitude of commitment to doing great things, while welcoming new people and fresh ideas. As your organization explores what "like me" looks like, you need to be mindful of not unconsciously creating any discrimination that would rob you of diverse ideas and experiences.

IDENTIFYING A CANDIDATE POOL AND MESSAGING TO THEM

Identifying the characteristics begins by looking closely at your existing team and then figuring out what's missing. These missing elements can be defined by the orientation defined by methodologies like DISC or Six Types of Working Genius (which you can google if they aren't familiar).

Sometimes the answer isn't obvious. For example, you might think that attention to detail and process are the most important characteristics for a Chief Financial Officer position, but not necessarily. At two organizations we work with, the most essential characteristic for CFOs are the people skills necessary to work with bankers and investors. Yes, they also need to have a grasp of financial detail and strong analytical ability, but these CFOs manage teams that are very detail-oriented and can analyze data. The essential work of making meaning from the data and communicating it externally is a different skill set.

After we identify those key characteristics, how do we apply that knowledge and our purpose and values into generating a candidate pool? The next step is the messaging you need to communicate to potential candidates. Organizations with a buy-in culture don't use generic messaging in their ads, recruitment emails, or LinkedIn posts. They know that unappealing messages will drive away the specific talent pool they are seeking.

Consider the difference between the website language of two companies competing for the same employees: Starbucks and Dutch Bros. Starbucks says: "Be more than an employee. Be a partner . . . part of something bigger."[6] It then has three sentences describing their purpose and values, but requires clicking a button to find out what they are. Dutch Bros, in contrast, boasts: "If you're ready to make a massive difference, we're stoked to talk to you!" It then goes on to promise an "opportunity to learn together, grow together and have a ton of fun doing it." The company's core values are listed in bold letters just below.[7] Guess which company has a turnover rate 50% lower than the other's, saving them millions in turnover, training, and productivity costs?[8]

Or consider Raising Cane's, a fast-food chicken chain that has been recognized as one of the best large employers by *Forbes* magazine over the past few years.[9] Their recruiting message boasts, "You can get a paycheck anywhere," listing "career training," "recognition & rewards," and having "fun on your path to success" as employee benefits.[10] Their top competitor, KFC, merely says, in bold letters, "Join our KFC family," and offers links on how to do it.[11] But what are the benefits of this supposed "KFC family"? If I want a food service job, why should I care? There are no compelling or clear answers on that recruiting page. Which company would appeal to you more if you were just starting out?

If your company's recruitment messages highlight pay, they will attract people who only focus on pay. You'll get a candidate pool that's willing to stay only as long as they can't find someone else who's willing to pay more. Since there is almost always an employer that pays more, and cyclical bidding wars as Jeff in Salt Lake City faced, you will face the scourge of high turnover. And even while those people work for you, values alignment will be a crapshoot. Maybe your applicants will have values that align with yours, but more likely not.

A BETTER WAY TO EVALUATE JOB CANDIDATES

The best predictor of future behavior is past behavior. So the next step is establishing a specific methodology to evaluate candidates, and training everyone who conducts interviews to use it. The key to finding the characteristics you need is *not* asking directly about those characteristics—it's asking about specific *behaviors* that correlate with those characteristics.

That's how great companies like Target conduct behavior-based interviews. To be fair to applicants, they inform them in advance how the interview will differ from the typical job interview, and they offer practice prompts so people can get comfortable with the format. (This lines up with Target's value of "equitable experiences for all.")[12]

So what does incorporating behavioral questions into the interview process look like? One practice we use with clients is to design questions tied directly to the organization's purpose and key values. For instance, a sample purpose question could be: "Our purpose is to improve the lives of millions. Can you think about a time you improved someone's life? What was the situation? What caused you to take action? What did you do? How did it make you feel?" The answers will indicate to what extent your company's purpose actually matters to the candidate. It might be easy to fake a general answer—"I care deeply about helping people"—but it's hard to fake specific details about how they actually practice that ideal.

Similarly, here's an example of how you might develop questions tied to values: "An important value for our company is integrity. Could you tell us about a time at work when you felt you were asked or told to do something that you believed was wrong? How did you respond? What did you do? What happened as a result? What did you learn?" The answers to these questions will provide the interviewer with clear signs about how that candidate is likely to behave in the future.

Or consider the Disney theme parks, which have the challenge of hiring thousands of seasonal workers every year. They prioritize a candidate's willingness to engage with other people, but they can't simply ask, "How do you feel about engaging with people?" Instead, they interview candidates two at a time. While one candidate is answering a question, the interviewer subtly checks the other candidate's reaction. Are they thinking about their own answer, daydreaming, or paying rapt attention to what the other person is saying? This skill of paying attention to others, particularly in high-stress situations, is exactly what a theme park needs when the crowds are huge and patrons are demanding.

Similarly, buy-in organizations are thoughtful about how they craft questions to uncover other personal characteristics. You can ask a candidate about their three greatest accomplishments, why they are important, and how they achieved them. Listen carefully to how they answer—are the details specific and clear? Or are you just getting vague generalities? This is especially important if attention to detail is an important characteristic for the position you are filling.

All of these question types about past behavior help predict how well candidates will fit into your culture and whether they will be good at doing what you need them to do. As you and your team refine your arsenal of questions, make sure you share them among every leader who conducts interviews, not just within the HR department.

PERFORMANCE AND CONTRIBUTION FEEDBACK

Let's turn now to performance and contribution feedback, the bane of countless employees and leaders alike. When done badly, these conversations can easily be an awkward, unpleasant waste of time. They become a ritualized dance of "Let me pay you a few compliments before hitting you with a vague list of deficiencies I want you to fix." And most of those alleged deficiencies are really just ways in which the reviewee approaches things differently from how the reviewer would do them.

But when done well, performance conversations can become a powerful opportunity to create and reinforce the Buy-In Advantage. They can drive candid, helpful discussions about behaviors, values, and true personal growth—not just advice to emulate the executive or team leader. And for leaders, these reviews can go from their least favorite activity to an easy, even pleasant, way to improve the quality of their team and strengthen a buy-in culture. Your team members are best placed to provide their own performance assessments—if properly equipped. Getting them fully prepared to assess themselves is one of the leader's roles, while another is to marshal resources to help their team members achieve their goals.

Contrast this approach with the old leadership model that goes back to the industrial revolution, when the average worker had a seventh-grade education and the average leader sought only obedience, not personal development. The subtext of every performance review was: "I know better than you and have a more important position, so I will tell you exactly what you are doing wrong and how to get better." Traditional performance reviews also create a paper trail for potential future dismissal, because that's what lawyers require. Or if the employee is doing well, the performance review becomes evidence toward a raise, on the assumption that more money is the only form of reward that counts. This model unfortunately became reinforced for generations in elementary education, when we were all assigned grades depending on how well we could deliver exactly what our teachers asked of us.

Research on performance feedback indicates that it's worth the time and effort to do well. Our firm's survey of thousands of employees shows that nearly 100% of highly engaged employees benefit from regular one-on-one meetings with their supervisors, "including authentic feedback to help me grow." In contrast, only one-third of employees who are less engaged report high quality feedback. In other words, leaders who are well-trained in effective performance reviews, and who make the time to hold constructive one-on-one sessions, end up with both better performance and more loyalty from their teams.

What does great feedback really look like? We've learned that it comes from what employees share about their aspirations and performance. For that to happen, the table needs to be set correctly before any review conversation actually begins.

SETTING THE TABLE FOR PERFORMANCE FEEDBACK

Asking employees to evaluate their own performance without all the relevant information in front of them is like tying one arm behind their backs and asking them to spar. It's unfair and gives all the advantages to the leader. Instead, setting the table for an effective performance conversation requires several other conversations in advance, to establish alignment on:

- What goals and priorities the team member should be aiming for.
- What metrics the team member can influence.
- What a great performance in this role looks like.
- What sources of information should be considered in evaluating performance.

The goals and priorities conversation may sound strange to anyone who is still stuck in the era of "my priorities are whatever the boss tells me to do." That model may create compliance, but it rarely leads to buy-in. You will get much better results when each team member has an opportunity to weigh in on how their department contributes to company goals, and to participate in discussions about setting objectives and who is responsible for achieving them. Even if a team member does not own a goal, they still contribute to one or more goals. Setting the table means helping them understand which goals they contribute to and how. It's up to the leader to confirm such understanding by asking the team member to repeat back what they understand their role to be. The same is true for metrics about what's being accomplished. How do a team member's daily activities contribute to various metrics?

Next, if "what great looks like" is in the eye of the beholder, the process is doomed. A two-way conversation needs to occur to set the table of what criteria will be used to evaluate performance. Consider: What is on your own checklist of what great looks like for a particular team member? Then share it with them, give them time to reflect, and ask for clarifying questions and any additional criteria you may have missed.

And be careful how you ask about what you missed. It may seem obvious to simply say, "What did I miss?" but that can lead to people clamming up. If the leader seems too incompetent to know the appropriate criteria, why should the employee set the bar any higher? Instead, you can add something like, "If we were going to add a few more items to this performance checklist, what might they be?"

Sources of information are the final area for setting the table. Does the team member have the same access to information that the person doing the evaluation has? If not, how can they get that access? One company I know does an informal survey of peers in other departments in order to prepare performance reviews. If that's something you'd consider, jointly identify how the team member can get access to the same information ahead of time.

Setting the table is an often overlooked yet important step in creating context before you start the actual performance feedback.

PERFORMANCE FEEDBACK CONVERSATIONS

After the table has been set, let the feedback begin! Best practice is that great feedback is constant, two way, and data driven. It is both scheduled and unscheduled. It occurs in meetings, in texts, on sticky notes, in team meetings, and on phone calls.

This means that there's a case for eliminating traditional annual reviews and replacing them with weekly meetings and continuous feedback. As noted above, annual assessments are widely disliked by all parties involved (except for company lawyers seeking a paper trail) and may feel like a nearly meaningless formality. Most of the time they are poorly done despite best efforts, because team leaders do not have sufficient training in how to do them well. They are usually forgotten quickly.

In contrast, weekly two-way conversations provide a continuous opportunity to:

- Deepen a mutual personal connection.
- Update each other on performance against the key objectives and metrics (keeping this part brief is fine, unless things are off track).
- Raise new issues for collaboration.
- Request new kinds of support or advice.

Once you have a standing weekly performance conversation on your calendar, try very hard never to cancel unless truly necessary. When you cancel just because you're busy with other business matters, you send the signal that those matters are more important than your team members.

The part of the conversation updating performance should be led by each team member. You may not need to say much unless you disagree with how the employee is describing their current performance.

If the leader perceives a performance issue not raised by the team member, there are several things to keep in mind. Underperformance is never the exclusive fault of one party. The person's leadership and surrounding system inevitably contributed to that miss. Therefore, a constructive attitude is to get curious and ask questions like: "What informs your assessment that this objective/measure is on track?" If you see the situation differently, ask a follow-up question: "If you were to consider X, how would that change your assessment?"

The goal for this discussion is uncovering a way to change future results. Are additional resources required? Should there be fewer priorities? Is training or another tool lacking? Telling someone they are not performing won't be necessary if the leader has been doing their job properly. They already know they have missed the mark. It's up to the leader to be a co-detective to get to the bottom of what went wrong and co-create a plan to fix it. The best fix will usually be one that the team member identifies on their own.

New issues may include questions or challenges that haven't come up before. This part of your one-on-one is a great chance to use the techniques of chapter 6: "Focus on Questions Instead of Answers." Your questions might include: "What options should we consider? How will we know which option is best? Is there additional information we need? How will that info inform this decision?" How the person responds to such questions and thinks about the situation will give you valuable information as you support their growth and development.

One myth about feedback is that telling people, "Good job!" is constructive. In my experience, I'd argue that it's actually destructive. If you are like most of us, you are doing a dozen things in a day. If someone says, "Good job!" you are left to wonder which of the things you are doing informed that compliment. Further, it makes you wonder if the other person even actually knows what you're doing. So, as a leader, if you ever feel like saying, "Good job!" tie it to a specific activity that relates to a specific measure or objective.

The best feedback comes from peers. Game-changing organizations set up regular opportunities for authentic peer recognition. Some invest in software that automates this kind of feedback and provides reward incentives for participating. While this is better than no peer feedback at all, it's better to create a process that feels more personal, authentic, and meaningful. Some companies create a physical feedback wall where employees can praise each other with posted notes. Some set up Slack channels for celebrating colleagues' accomplishments. Others set aside time in every meeting to celebrate someone else's accomplishments. However you encourage lateral feedback, remember that it will probably be appreciated more than any recognition a leader can offer.

CONTRIBUTION FEEDBACK CONVERSATIONS

One of the hallmarks of a buy-in culture is that people know what they are doing is important and that the organization cares about their personal growth goals. While relevancy is established through alignment with purpose, it's up to the leader to take the time to understand what growth and opportunity mean in the eyes of each individual team member. What do they really enjoy doing? Where do they want to be in five years? What training or support can the organization provide to help them get there?

These conversations can make leaders squirm if someone's goals involve something the organization can't support. For example, one client in corporate aviation kept losing pilots to Southwest and Delta. We suggested that instead of hiding that those team members were leaving for better paying jobs at bigger companies, our client ought to celebrate them. We encouraged management to be proud that some of their best pilots were later recruited by the big guys, and to use this trend as a selling point for new recruits. "Hey, some of our best alumni move on to the major carriers. If you eventually want to be with a major carrier, we can give you a big advantage. They look to us as a proven training ground. Come with us for three years and we'll get you ready."

With that attitude in mind, we suggest doing such conversations once a quarter. How is the team member proceeding in their growth and moving toward their personal goals? What's working? What's not? If the employee has mastered their existing role, you can explore additional opportunities for cross-functional teamwork or special projects that could further their skills and career.

This is also a great opportunity to ask them to reflect on ways they are contributing to the greater good at the company, whether via assisting others, promoting the culture, identifying new opportunities, or going above and beyond in some other way. Whatever they offer, you have the opportunity to ask how that effort relates to a company goal or value and express appreciation.

A contribution feedback conversation should be done in a half hour or less. While it doesn't have to be a long exchange, it's very important.

CONNECTING STRATEGIC PLANS WITH PEOPLE

Another hallmark of companies that have the Buy-In Advantage is that every person in the organization knows how important what it is they are doing. When team members feel heard as part of the planning process, magic happens because they are vested as part owners. Yet having every team member involved in all planning results in chaos.

When strategic plans are shared, it's time for leaders to step into action with their teams. Share the priorities ahead of time and allow team members to consider: What strategy affects us and what can we affect? What would we start, stop, or double down on doing as a result? Are there resources we need to contribute to this strategy?

Go through the ideation session outlined in chapter 7 and then boil down the top handful of strategies you want to pursue with your team this quarter. Of course, there may be others you're eager to add, but remember that "three is better than seven." Having too many priorities is just as bad as having no priorities at all. For each strategy, identify if the existing metrics your team uses are sufficient or if there are other measures you will need to consider during the quarter ahead.

Identify owners, measures, and evidence for each strategy. There can only be one owner for each; that person isn't responsible for executing the strategy, but is accountable for making sure it's accomplished. They become like a player-coach, doing some things themselves while coaching others to accomplish the rest, checking in frequently and holding contributors accountable. The owner can do a weekly assessment of whether the team is on track to execute the strategy or if help is needed. A weekly check-in with the entire team will promote buy-in for all involved.

As strategies are accomplished or measures met, celebrate! This could be as simple as offering congratulations, making an announcement in a broader setting, giving gift cards, granting extra time off, or whatever is important to your team. If you forget or neglect to celebrate, people may wonder if the effort was worth the pain.

Is it okay to add strategies in the middle of a quarter? Ideally not, because that defeats the purpose of learning how to systematically prioritize strategies from quarter to quarter. At the end of each quarterly discussion, you will be looking for takeaways on how your team could have chosen different strategies or communicated yours more effectively. If you change the strategy willy-nilly during the quarter, you will eliminate this learning opportunity. So save that move for very occasional, truly urgent situations.

What about individual objectives as opposed to team objectives? Every single person in the organization should be able to tell you how their work directly contributes to at least one specific departmental or organizational strategy and the measure that reflects their activities. We hear from executives regularly who feel frustrated because they get feedback on how they are doing something instead of what they are accomplishing. You can check each person's clarity and comprehension of what's important about their contribution by simply asking, "What's most important for you to accomplish this quarter?" Recognize that it could be a metric, an objective, a behavior change (to better line up with values), or an activity linked to the team's well-being.

Ideas Worth Considering

1. What messaging do we provide potential applicants? Does it communicate our culture, purpose, and advantages of working with us beyond money and benefits?

2. What about our interview process is working well? What changes can we make to add critical questions?

3. How do we measure the quantity and quality of authentic feedback sessions? Do we have training for leaders in how to let talent lead a self-evaluation? How do we offer support for an individual's growth plan?

Chapter 13

ADOPT MODELING, CASCADING, AND CELEBRATING TO REINVIGORATE BUY-IN

A friend told me a story about a CEO who had successfully built a company from scratch to almost $40 million in revenue. His biggest problem was that he ran through executives like a track team, and complained that those he hired never quite measured up to what he expected. At executive meetings he'd put a chart on the screen with about 50 different metrics. The CEO would open the meeting and dominate the discussion, grilling his team on why objectives fell short. None of those attending ever knew which metric would draw his focus that day. It was as if the CEO were a searchlight in a dark room, illuminating different areas each time. Without discussion he would then add five or six additional ideas on what should be done and by when.

In private, the CEO complained his executives were lazy or were "just not getting it." Also in private, his direct reports complained about too many priorities that shifted too often and came with too few resources to tackle properly. They felt sorry for the person being grilled at any given meeting and thanked their lucky stars when it wasn't them. They also said they were given so many ideas to pursue that it was up to them to prioritize. God help them if the ideas they didn't prioritize were the ones he asked about.

This stressful, miserable culture led to higher turnover below the executive team as well. The behavior that CEO modeled—"Do what I say, not what I do"—trickled down. Most people learn how to lead by observing more senior leaders, for better or worse. In this case, it was the exact opposite of what would be required to move the company to the next level and create stability.

Although it's easy to listen to this story and quickly criticize this CEO for all the things he did "wrong," his mentors (if he had any) probably didn't share with him the three leadership habits that can maintain a culture of buy-in: *modeling*, *cascading*, and *celebrating*.

Modeling requires practicing the behaviors you want to see in your people, rather than holding them to a morale-wrecking "Do what I say, not what I do" standard. Done correctly and consistently, modeling shows the entire organization what buy-in-focused leadership looks like.

Cascading is the art of being explicit about what you want done, and sharing the necessary information about a new strategy or tactic, along with clarity about its purpose. Done well through a company's hierarchy, cascading enables even frontline employees and new hires to understand and accept the purpose, goals, and metrics of a new policy or plan.

Celebrating is different from merely recognizing the accomplishment of financial targets or other metrics. It's about taking the time and energy to deliberately call out positive behaviors, especially when people have been working together to accomplish great things. Making people feel seen, heard, and appreciated releases dopamine, which encourages them to keep doing more things that will be worth celebrating.

Practicing all three consistently will make it increasingly likely that employees:

- Know the company's purpose and use it to help fuel their performance.
- Understand strategic priorities and how they impact their day-to-day work.

- Feel empowered to share their ideas and solutions.
- Feel comfortable asking for the help they need to overcome obstacles.

The three habits will also help leaders sleep better, knowing they have created an environment that encourages everyone to contribute their full selves to achieving the organization's goals.

Habit One: Modeling

There's a common pattern that leaders often fall into, which I call the "tell-do" loop.

Leaders answer problems from team members and tell them what to do. It's usually well intended, and when we talk to those leaders we hear some version of: "I won't be here forever so if I tell them what to do, they will catch on and hopefully be as good as me." The challenge is that no one will ever be as "good" as you, or as "bad" as you. You are you and they are them. Teaching someone by telling them what to do is not allowing them to learn; it's asking them to copy you.

Admittedly, there's a fine line between telling someone what to do and modeling what they should do. But it's a crucial distinction. What truly enables others to learn is to encourage them to develop their own critical thinking skills. This has to be done by listening and asking questions to help the other person clarify their thinking, not just blindly copy whatever you're doing. They will learn mainly via experience, not by copying you. In the future, when you are not there to address problems, these critical thinking skills will serve your people well. So you need to embed them into your culture.

What to emphasize as you model leadership will vary based on the size of the company, its existing culture, and what the business demands. No two leaders will do things exactly the same way. So it's up to you to make conscious choices about what to model based on what your business needs.

Are you like the CEO who was so overscheduled he ran from meeting to meeting, and when people tried to stop him in the hall he'd yell, "Not now—can you talk to me later?" In most cases, later never came. He was both cut off from important input and did not have a chance to share his experience or model best practices. He would have been far better off to schedule breaks in between his meetings, to make time for chance encounters and respond to urgent calls or emails. He missed his chance to model being available and approachable.

When it comes to modeling, there are three daily practices we see leaders employ regularly that strengthen a buy-in culture: vision and values storytelling, leveraging others' strengths, and deep listening at skip-level meetings. Let's look at each.

Vision and Values Storytelling

For thousands of years humans gathered around a fire together to build trust, understanding, and social bonds. Vision and values storytelling continues this tradition in a business setting. The simple idea is that a story can bring to life the purpose, values, and meaning of the work to be done—often more powerfully than declaring them as statements.

For instance, in the early days of Federal Express, every employee could tell the story of the desperation of founder Fred Smith. The company grew rapidly and burned through its $80 million funding. With only $5,000 in the bank and bankruptcy days away, Smith went to Las Vegas and gambled, winning $27,000—enough to keep the company alive. It remains an example of pursuing innovative (if risky!) solutions and never giving up under adversity.[1]

At any company, vision and values storytelling can be done in small group settings, newsletters, or town hall meetings. It can be as simple as telling the story of the actions or decisions of one team member and tying them to the values or vision of the company. This might sound like: "When Sally did [action X] it really demonstrated [our value Y]. I'm so proud of her." Correctly done, such storytelling is a powerful reminder of what's important and how it shows up in the daily practices of the organization.

One mistake we sometimes see is that this recognition only goes to a member of senior management, or only to longtime employees. This risks being demotivating instead of instructive. It also unintentionally suggests that the only people worth recognizing are senior leaders or long-termers, as if they are the only ones doing the important stuff!

Leveraging Others' Strengths

At organizations where people have buy-in, everyone's opinion is respected.

This does not mean that everyone gets to vote on every decision. But it does mean that, in healthy organizations, sharing different points of view and different experiences at all levels is a culture norm. And leadership needs to reinforce that norm constantly.

This attitude requires an honest and humble recognition of what you are *not* good at as a leader. Most leaders easily recognize their strengths but sometimes struggle to recognize those areas in which others are better. They are likely to say, "I've got this," even if someone else on the team is more qualified to take the lead.

At the other end of the spectrum are leaders who feel uncertain about themselves or their teams and bring in outsiders to serve as saviors. This kind of leader will hire someone from a successful competitor or much larger, name-brand organization, assuming they will come with whatever answers or formulas made their previous employer successful. This inadvertently brings (often silent) resentment from existing team members, who feel insulted or undervalued, and sets up unrealistic expectations that usually result in failure.

Leaders who are able to leverage others' strengths are okay with saying, "I don't know" or, "Who is really good at this? I need assistance!" Remember from chapter 9 the story of CEO Jeremy Levitt turning over executive meeting facilitation to a team member who had better skills at running meetings? It all comes down to gap analysis in both people and processes. Leaders who recognize both their strengths and weaknesses have a talent for hiring people different from themselves instead of those in their own likeness. Particularly in sales, we often see VPs hire in their own likeness at the expense of getting the best results.

Fortunately, there are simple tools to easily identify people with different strengths and assemble balanced teams with different skills and orientations. Patrick Lencioni's "Six Types of Working Genius" is one way to identify what people are more oriented toward doing well. His six types include people with imagination, the ability to bring people together, and tenacity. He argues that all six are required for a highly effective team.[2] You can also use DISC profiles as another way to identify people's orientation on two dimensions: people versus data and the pace at which they work.

Highly effective leaders find numerous ways to model how they seek out assistance. For instance, when the company faces an important issue, the leader can assemble a cross-functional team built around people with different strengths. Note that different *strengths* is a different concept than simply tapping people from different *departments*. You could assemble a team of detail-oriented analysts from multiple departments and satisfy a cross-functional requirement, while missing the benefit of assembling a team with different strengths.

Another great option is seeking help from a wider network of like-minded leaders. This might include forums such as YPO, EO, or Vistage; industry leadership groups; or a personal advisory network of relationships you've built over the years. However you seek out others who are competent in different ways than you are, you will make an impact by modeling the power of leveraging others' strengths.

Deep Listening at Skip-Level Sessions

Deep listening is a powerful habit developed and practiced by leaders who don't feel the need to have all the answers or show off how smart they are. They would rather focus on asking the right questions (as we covered in chapter 6) and directing them to the right people (not just their own direct reports). These leaders don't get caught in the echo chamber of the executive suite. Nor do they allow themselves to be held prisoner by a misguided open-door policy, which puts the burden on team members who have something valuable to say to show up at that door.

When Kent Thiry took over Total Renal Care, it was a broken-down kidney dialysis company on the verge of bankruptcy. He led a major turnaround (and rebranding as DaVita), in part by focusing on deep listening to frontline workers who had been ignored by the previous leadership. Kent modeled taking time from his schedule each month to meet with the newest incoming "class" of team members, to personally share the company's vision and values and get to know them. This was part of a strategy to align energies and increase retention, which led to vastly lower turnover and increased productivity and profitability.[3]

Equally impactful are leaders who get out of the corporate office and visit the factory floor or different locations. The presence of leadership sends a strong message even if no words are spoken. Some leaders we talk with say, "Oh, I wish I had time to do that." Every leader knows they have time for anything they choose. And, by choosing how they spend their time, leaders are telegraphing without words what is important to them. When Scott Beck was CEO of CHG, he would schedule time every year for visits to many locations to connect. When he was in the office, he would eat in the company lunchroom every day. Instead of sitting with the same people, he would purposefully pick a table and sit with employees he did not know.

You'll note that I specified "skip level" sessions as especially key for deep listening. When I was CEO of a multinational company, I found it massively helpful and inspiring to meet for an hour with small groups of people several layers below me on the org chart, without their supervisors present. At first, some of their leaders saw this practice as a threat, as if I were using these meetings to dig up dirt on them via their frontline people. But that wasn't my goal at all. In fact, whenever someone in the room raised a concern about their leader or a colleague, I'd redirect them to talk to that person directly about the problem. The purpose of these sessions wasn't for me to interfere in any department's day-to-day challenges or conflicts. Had I tried to interfere or even to serve as a mediator or messenger, that would have been a recipe for increasing dysfunction rather than building trust.

I was always surprised when people in these sessions didn't know each other, or if they only had a history of treating each other as human doings rather than human beings. We always began with introductions, including a question that gave a taste of their personality, such as, "What are you celebrating in your life?" After that initial connection, I'd ask, "What's going well?" and, "What can we improve on?" Inevitably, one member of the group would offer to assist another in addressing an issue without me having to do anything. I'd also include one of my favorite questions: "If you were our CEO, what would you do differently?" My response to any ensuing criticism was always, "Thank you."

In an earlier chapter we met Jeff Edison, CEO of Phillips Edison. Jeff is a gifted leader and one of the smartest people I know. He's quick to evaluate new ideas and apply them when they make sense. When I observed him in action, I noted that he's one of the rare leaders who waits to speak last. This allows others to share their ideas freely without worrying whether or not it lines up with what the leader was thinking. Today, Jeff invests effort to create thoughtful questions to tap into the best thinking of others. He knows he learns more from listening than speaking. He asks his people to speak first—and not because he's playing a "guess what the leader is thinking" game. It is truly about his interest in hearing a diversity of opinions.

Like vision and values storytelling and leveraging others' strengths, deep listening via skip-level meetings costs virtually nothing—but it models to everyone that their voices matter and their work is appreciated and respected.

Habit Two: Cascading

When you were a kid, did you play the telephone game? A group of people line up and whisper a message one at a time to the person next to them. Inevitably, a complicated message changes a little with each retelling. When the last person announces what they think it said, and then the first reveals what they actually tried to communicate, the disconnect is often hilarious.

Cascading is a leadership tool that solves the business equivalent of the telephone game. Think of it as a waterfall of ideas or important information flowing through an organization, without distortion. This enables leaders to get their key messages out quickly to every level of the organization—and, more importantly, have them acted on! (Technically, this is called "cascading vertically." Another variation is "cascading horizontally" across departments, which we'll discuss later in the book.)

Consultant Patrick Lencioni has observed that one role that leaders need to embrace is that of "Chief Repeating Officer"—because people need to be exposed to messages multiple times before they truly sink in.[4] Research suggests that adults may need to hear something *seven times* to get it "in their bones." Successful leaders know that each person has one of three primary learning styles: auditory, visual, or kinesthetic. They consider how to deliver key messages in memorable ways across different platforms to address these learning styles. The really good ones make the message still seem fresh and sincere with each repetition, like a rock star singing their hit song for the thousandth time.

Delivery from the heart will always beat reading a message from a script. Your goal for each message is to show why it's important, provide relevant context, and link it to your purpose and values.

At one client, the CEO spent months with his team, crafting a budget that reflected their key priorities for the upcoming year. To really make the messaging stick, we built on the usual approach of a company-wide email and town hall announcement by adding:

- A video via WhatsApp and Telegraph for visual learners.
- A voicemail announcement for auditory learners.
- Posters about the new budget that could be easily seen around the office.
- Additional messaging from all department heads in small group meetings, with opportunities for everyone to ask questions.

These approaches covered everyone except the kinesthetic learners, who learn by doing. Telling people something or showing them something is not impactful for those who are primarily kinesthetic learners. How could we get them to participate in the new corporate strategy launch? We came up with a powerful way to vertically cascade for kinesthetic learners: call a team together, share the strategy, then facilitate a discussion about how it would impact that specific team. What would they need to start, stop, or double down on doing as a result of the strategy? What else did they need to know? Were any additional training or tools necessary to effectively execute the strategy? Responding to these questions allowed kinesthetic learners to fully absorb the message and put it into action.

So, when do you know that your message has been heard? Only when you share it (yet again!) several levels below you, and people can finish your sentences for you. Until then, keep practicing your role as Chief Repeating Officer (CRO)!

Habit Three: Celebrating

In too many organizations, celebration is an afterthought at best. It's "Oh yeah, let's drop her an email and say, 'Good work!'" As noted earlier, such general praise may be well intentioned, but it comes with unintended consequences. Just as we stress tying specific actions to values, you always need to be specific about what you're celebrating.

We also stress the importance of celebrating people as human beings, not just human doings. After explaining this distinction, I once asked a group of leaders running a nationwide company how they recognize human beings. One of them replied, "We hand out Visa gift cards when people exceed their numbers!" This recognition is fine for human doings (accomplishments) but likely to have no impact on human beings (behaviors and choices). In contrast, imagine a department head who says, "I recognize that you had to travel Tuesday for a client and you missed your child's performance at school. I appreciate that you made that sacrifice and want to plan further ahead next time, so this won't be a regular occurrence. I know how important it is to you to be there for them." That's cheaper than a Visa gift card but far more valuable!

Celebration is most impactful when it occurs in different ways, at different times, in different mediums. Recognizing all team members with May birthdays each year is well intentioned yet becomes predictable and easily ignored. Imagine all the other ways to recognize human beings! Leaders who take time to create celebrations send an important message about what's worth doing and how it's worth doing. Successful celebrations are inspired and address three distinct dimensions: who is to be celebrated, how to recognize those people, and when a celebration should be held. Some questions you can ask yourself as you ponder celebration options:

- *Should we recognize individual behaviors or team behaviors?* "Teams" can include shifts, departments, divisions, or an entire company. And remember that teams can also include cross-functional collaborators who get stuff done together. But also keep in mind that some cultures stress individual performance, such as highly driven sales organizations. If people see their work as individual, their rewards should mostly be individual as well. Other organizations are all about teams.

- *What's a creative delivery mechanism that can make celebration special?* Consider how you would celebrate a loved one's accomplishments. Would you send them an email or text? Probably not! So what's more meaningful and memorable? Some leaders even get vulnerable and dress up in costumes to make the point.

- *When should we celebrate?* Is it best to wait for a quarterly town hall? A weekly staff meeting? Or a surprise moment that no one sees coming?

- *Are we repeating the same kind of celebration too often?* No one enjoys getting the same old, same old. You might love lobster, but it would quickly lose its appeal if you had to eat it every night!

The same is true for special moments at work that stop being special.

Here are some of my favorite examples of getting creative with celebrations:

- Aero-Graphics recognizes team accomplishments by taking a couple-hour break from work with a gourmet food truck. It's a different one every time, so people can wonder what kind of great food will be available this time.
- Jerry Seiner Dealerships, a multi-state car dealer, celebrates local dealerships by having leaders from headquarters show up and serve as barbecue chefs for a cookout.
- Some companies send out texts or WhatsApp messages to recognize accomplishments. They are a lot less formal than emails, and you can easily enhance the message with a picture of the person or team being celebrated. A video is even better!
- Barry Schlouch of Schlouch Inc. recognizes company celebrations on the company's LinkedIn page, so all of the honoree's connections can see the good news.
- Paul Baribault, president and CEO of the San Diego Zoo Wildlife Alliance, also creates eye-catching LinkedIn posts that include sharp graphics and inspire his team and readers about the organization's potential of what they can achieve together.
- One client celebrated beating their targets by setting up a dunking tank in the parking lot. People could take turns throwing balls at the tank to sink their senior executives. That was far more memorable than the typical office party!
- Numerous clients have adopted personal, handwritten notes of celebration, sent to employees at their homes so family members can see them too. This is even more effective if the note comes with a simple gift. Once, when my own company launched an incentive contest, with the top prize a Caribbean vacation, we sent everyone the contest rules at home with a small tube of sunscreen.

One more dimension that you need to consider is the ideal time frame in between an accomplishment and its celebration. The right answer will vary by organization. Some employees need to be recognized immediately for doing something outstanding, for the sake of positive reinforcement. Some teams are used to getting monthly or quarterly metrics about their results, in which case those might be appropriate milestones for recognition and celebration. Still other cultures are geared around annual results, such as a sales force with a big annual prize for best overall performance.

Again, variety is better than stagnation. Naming someone "customer service rep of the month" is well intended but can quickly become boring and ineffective if the process never changes. Instead, what if you highlight a different dimension of customer service every month, and announce the special dimension in advance as a motivator? Or you can change who does the selecting every month, with different employees taking turns as evaluators (with well-defined criteria, so it's not just a popularity contest). Another option is to let everyone at a monthly or quarterly gathering call out nominations for who they think deserves the honor that time.

You can even gamify your celebrations. One client incentivizes salespeople by giving them a ticket for a prize drawing each time they sell or conduct a specific activity, such as generating a new lead. At the end of the month they hold the drawing, and those who have the most tickets have the greatest odds of winning.

Ideally you should vary your awards as well, to keep celebrations exciting. They may include cash, gift cards, time off, or experiences. If building a team is important, consider a team experience that will include going to an activity together during business hours. Consider including families in some celebrations, such as a bowling party. The options are truly limitless if you use your imagination.

Like modeling and cascading, healthy forms of celebrating don't have to be expensive, but they can pay off with a huge impact on buy-in. Effective leaders know that these habits aren't about adding more work to their to-do lists, but about proving the importance of people to the organization. When practiced regularly, these habits drive more initiative, a more positive environment, and a stronger bottom line.

HOW CRYSTAL SAVED HER FAMILY BUSINESS

Let's end this chapter with an inspiring example of putting these techniques into practice. Crystal Maggelet is a hardworking, unassuming, yet highly accomplished entrepreneur. Her dad, Jay Call, was a successful startup founder who nudged Crystal to use her Harvard MBA to start something new instead of taking some corporate middle management job. When the Olympics were coming to their hometown of Salt Lake City, Jay recognized a need for mid-priced, clean, safe hotels and urged Crystal to build that business, which she did with great success (perhaps you've stayed at a Crystal Inn Hotel).

A few years later, Crystal spent more time focusing on raising her four children, while her father hired a CEO to run the family holding company, which included the Flying J convenience and fuel chain, insurance, convenience stores, and other sectors. Crystal remained on the company's board.

Then, tragically, Jay died in a plane crash. Not long after, Crystal was shocked to learn that the CEO was about to file for bankruptcy! The big problem was that working capital for a major expansion had been secured by the company's oil assets, and oil prices had just collapsed by two-thirds. Crystal had the board fire the CEO and returned to the business full-time. Crystal later recalled, "I went from being a stay-at-home mom to CEO of Flying J."[5] She went to every single bank who had lent to the company, promising to repay every cent if they could avoid bankruptcy. That seemed audacious, but she was extremely persuasive.

She also met with the management team and told them things were going to be different from then on. They would start doing the opposite of everything they had been doing. Symbolically, the previous CEO required everyone to wear ties, but Crystal instituted a "no tie" rule. More substantively, she recognized that the company had gotten into trouble by chasing revenue. As the turnaround worked, revenue *dropped* by 30%, but cash flow and profit improved dramatically. And people loved the new culture, with Crystal's emphasis on listening to the people closest to the work to figure out the best plan to make things better in each business unit. She later wrote a book about the transformation: *Building Value to Last*.

If your organization loses momentum or takes a wrong turn, it doesn't require *everything* to be done differently. A thoughtful analysis of what's working and what's not can give you an accurate map of both where you are and where you want to go. Then you, too, can decide what you need to model, cascade, and celebrate in your day-to-day activities, to build and sustain a culture grounded in buy-in.

Ideas Worth Considering

1. Do we have common stories often repeated that communicate our compelling purpose? What is our opportunity to make them even more known?
2. What are the most important messages we should be cascading now? How are we cascading our values?
3. What methods do we or could we successfully use to generate celebrations at all levels of the organization?

Chapter 14

APPLY COLLECTIVE GENIUS TO STRATEGIC PLANNING

"If you want to go fast, go alone. If you want to go far, go together."
—African proverb

I love that proverb because it aligns with my experiences as a CEO during the dreaded process of creating annual or quarterly strategic plans. I found that the more people were involved in the process, the longer it took and the more cumbersome it felt. It was much easier to just do planning with a small handful of trusted executives, or even all by myself. But the more people I included, the more likely we were to actually achieve the goals we were setting.

I hope you will recall Collective Genius from chapter 4 and elsewhere in this book. This chapter now shows the unique value of expanding this powerful mindset to include strategic planning. I recently got a reminder of that power from one of my clients.

CCI Mechanical is a leader in Utah in the design, installation, and maintenance of mechanical systems for commercial and industrial sites. For years they had created three-year strategic plans by gathering their top leaders for discussions about what needed to get done. That process worked well enough, but as they grew, CEO Dave Engel needed more regular and consistent ways to tap into the insights of his people.

My firm helped CCI adopt our Strategic Alignment and Accountability System, which we developed to apply Collective Genius specifically to strategic planning. The team at CCI embraced its concepts with open minds and curiosity. They leaned into it, even when they felt unsure. With time and effort, the cross-functional collaboration you'll soon learn about resulted in synergies between departments that CCI had never experienced before and could barely even imagine. Even more helpful for buy-in, the company's departments were able to successfully check their egos at the door. Department heads stopped seeing strategic planning as "my idea against your idea" and started to build on each other's ideas to tap the best elements of everyone's expertise.

Just a year into revising their strategic planning process, CCI was celebrating some of their strongest-ever results, including the largest single order they had ever received. CEO Engel updated me via email: "We've always had a culture of working hard and making progress, but we have come so far in the last year. We're more productive and efficient. We're getting the *big, important* things done and we're holding each other accountable."

Even though in-depth strategic planning happens less often than other functions we've covered in this book—typically once a year—it's important enough to deserve an approach centered on buy-in. When different perspectives are brought into the strategic planning process and the Collective Genius of the organization is properly harnessed, the impact can be tremendous. Instead of stoking rivalries between the leaders of various departments or business units, the planning process can nurture cross-functional groups that make various areas of the organization feel like a single team.

WHY DOES STRATEGIC PLANNING USUALLY DISAPPOINT?

Unlike CCI, most organizations do a "meh" job at best of both devising and executing their strategic plans. I say this without judgment, having been a leader at several companies where our strategic planning left a lot to be desired. There are three primary reasons for this tendency that I've observed:

- Strategic plans are devised in ways that make many people in the room lack any sense of buy-in.
- The plans are then communicated to everyone *outside* the room in ways that don't result in buy-in.
- Any enthusiasm or excitement about new plans fades quickly as day-to-day challenges grab everyone's attention. Before long, the new plan is forgotten.

The first two are the most challenging problems. If you can get everyone—both inside and outside the planning room—to feel genuine buy-in about new plans, it's a lot easier to hold their enthusiasm over time with a regular process for check-ins and accountability.

So the big question is why people often lack buy-in after the traditional planning process. Here are some of the most common reasons, which I bet you'll recognize from your own experiences:

- The strategic plan was designed purely to hit budget targets to satisfy investors or a parent company. It's hard to get excited about just hitting the budget!
- The planning process doesn't include any linkage between business goals, purpose, and values.
- The group that shapes the strategy is widely seen as too small, too insular, and too remote from the actual challenges of the front lines. (In other words, it goes against the principle of "All of us are smarter than any of us.")
- The overall plan is built up from the sub-plans of each department—but those departments are all focused on their own interests rather than the greater good.
- The language in the strategic plan is vague, lacks clear metrics, or is open to interpretation.

We designed our strategic planning process to solve for all of these problems—especially the lack of alignment across departments and the lack of accountability. It features four key steps:

- **Map.** Instead of beginning with your financial targets and working backward, begin by creating a map of your goals using the Collective Genius Process.
- **Test.** Test the meaning of strategies with people not involved in their creation, to ensure clarity and avoid misinterpretation or poor execution.
- **Activate.** Activate the plan by engaging team members in every department to make it their own and identify horizontal linkages.
- **Learn.** Use Collective Genius to learn from the results before creating the next plan.

Start with a Map So You Can Create a Better Plan

Most organizations I know start the planning process with an overall budget or financial target that's then broken up into subgoals. Department heads and other execs are given their numbers for the upcoming year and are asked how they can achieve those metrics. Their answers are discussed with senior management, modified as needed, written up as formal plans, and then distributed as the Official Plan.

The problem with this approach is that it works backward. It starts with revenue and profit goals and tries to figure out how to achieve them, instead of thinking holistically about what the business can accomplish and what would define greatness for the upcoming year. If you only focus on hitting the budget targets set by the company's investors or owners, what's truly possible gets tossed to the wayside. As Don Draper once said on *Mad Men*: "Who's in charge? A bunch of accountants trying to turn $1 into $1.10?" That mindset won't excite anyone. (No disrespect to my accountant friends!)

A different approach is to begin with this question: "What can we do that would radically improve our results year after year?" In other words, start with some blue sky brainstorming that might lead to 10x improvements, rather than (at best) 10% upward bumps in revenue. Create a formal process to THINK BIG.

We ask clients to create a map of what their world looks like. The map metaphor is useful because generating game-changing results is a journey, and any journey requires knowing your starting point. Then, when you agree where you want to go, the map shows the path forward. Along the journey you can look both forward and backward, as your performance serves as a reference point to celebrate progress.

The first step in creating this map is to align everyone on the current realities of the business. Using the Collective Genius Process, each member of the planning team addresses fundamental questions on their own, before discussing them with anyone else. Typical questions asked include:

- What's working? What's not?
- What economic factors are currently affecting us?
- What's changing with our customers, competition, regulation, or suppliers?
- Where are there new opportunities?
- How are we leaning into our values and our purpose?
- Are we on track to achieve our long-term goals?
- What are the issues that keep getting in our way, year after year?
- What have we learned from prior strategy successes and failures?

You can begin generating buy-in even before the plan is created by posing these same questions to people deep into the organization. When they know that their opinions will count, they are more likely to be engaged in whatever strategies result.

Collect and analyze the results, looking for patterns. This data will become important information for the executive team that will actually propose new strategies. They will learn not only how frontline employees and mid-level leaders perceive their world but where there are opportunities for improvement.

The next step in creating a map is to begin work on the destination. The strategy team turns to the question of "What is critically important that we get right as an overall organization in the next several years?" This is often a challenge for leaders because they are caught up in their specific departments or areas of expertise. This question asks them to think more broadly, like an outside observer of the entire business.

You'll likely come up with lots of ideas that need to be listed out. Look for duplicates or ideas that are close enough that they can be combined. Then prioritize the ideas by voting on them, with each team member allocating multiple votes as we discussed in chapter 4. Your goal is to end up with four or five short descriptions of major organizational goals that have significant support.

One reason this process works is that it doesn't challenge any one leader's domain over their own area or tell them what to do on a granular level. Instead, it's a collaborative process to identify what the whole company *as a collective* should do.

What's Critical for Us to Get Right?

I've found success using an exercise that asks the team to think about an unrelated industry, to help clear away any biases about their own industry. For instance, we often ask execs to pretend they are the C-suite of an airline. On their own, each has to answer the "What's critical for us to get right?" question. Their answers usually focus on:

- Customer experience (What's the customer journey like?)
- Safety (How do we minimize safety incidents?)
- Capacity (Do we have the right routes?)
- Timeliness (Is our on-time record hurting our reputation?)
- Employee experience (Do our people feel buy-in so they can create great customer experiences?)
- Fuel costs (How do we manage the unpredictable market price of jet fuel?)

When we conduct the same exercise using Amazon as the example, the results are completely different. Typically, the execs will now focus on:

- Logistics (How quickly can we deliver orders accurately?)
- Web experience (How many clicks does it take to find what you want and buy it?)
- Selection and availability (How often are customers frustrated by failed searches or out-of-stock messages?)
- Merchant relations (Can we attract and retain the suppliers we need?)
- Subscriptions (Can we entice more customers to pay for Amazon Prime?)

The results of this exercise will be different for any company you pick, even those in the same industry. And more importantly, each of these answers about critical areas involves *more than one department!* That's the key takeaway for your own team—they have to think beyond their own usual frame of reference.

For instance, let's consider the airline's priorities for capacity and timeliness. To get the right number of flights between two markets, and to have those flights take off and land on time, requires multiple parts of an airline working in harmony. The people team must make sure there are enough pilots, flight attendants, mechanics, gate agents, baggage handlers, customer service agents, and ramp people available at the right places and times. The planning team must accurately analyze demand and match the right aircraft to each route so there won't be too many empty seats or too many overbooked flights. The training department must ensure that pilots and flight attendants are meeting government and airline standards for current expertise. The purchasing department must make sure there is adequate fuel at each airport at the best available price. And so on.

Running this exercise will teach your people to approach planning with a *holistic* view of the organization and what it needs to get right, rather than a *narrow* view of a single department's goals and metrics.

Expand with Descriptors

When you've completed what we call "headline goals" in one or two words, it's time to create four or five short descriptors for each holistic headline. For example, under web experience at Amazon you might see:

- Server available and latency.
- Logic of links for fewest clicks.
- Easy access to alternatives and reviews.
- Great display on multiple-sized screens.

Now you will have an aligned list of what's critical to get right, with some bulleted details. This road map is *not* your strategic plan, but it will serve as an important reference document to inform everyone's brainstorming. The actual strategic plan will describe how to address these areas of improvement to generate potential 10x results.

Use this map as a reference point before each annual and quarterly planning session, and consider what is not being addressed that could be prioritized in the next planning cycle. This map is also a great tool to establish cross-functional teams to focus on each priority area.[1] You only need to revisit it every couple of years if the business changes significantly.

Now that you've created your map and used the Collective Genius Process to create potential strategies, it's time to test them out!

Test the Clarity and Practicality of Your Strategies

The wording of strategies is one of the invisible barriers that can prevent successful execution. So much time and attention can be focused on selecting each strategy, yet wording is often an afterthought. The team inside the planning room might know exactly what they meant by a word or phrase that will confuse or baffle many on the outside. Letting people reach different conclusions based on "the eye of the beholder" is fine for art museums or movie reviews, but not for strategic planning!

There is an art to expressing your plans in ways that provide guidance without stifling expertise in steps involved in execution. The more open to interpretation your plans are, the less likely they will be executed successfully. This is especially true when multiple parts of the organization are required for successful execution. So the first part of testing the strategy is for the team creating it to make sure that any third party reading it will be very clear on what's to be done.

For instance, let's say your strategy as stated is to "increase sales by 10%." Seems obvious, right? Well, some might take that to mean increasing unit volume by 10%, while others will think it means increasing revenue. Either group might conclude that any rising costs don't matter in achieving this goal, so they might start eroding profit margins via special discounts, new packaging, hiring additional salespeople, investing in new channels of distribution, or some other method. What will happen if you hit that 10% increase in units or revenue, but profits actually drop in the process?

The next step is to take the strategy to the departments that will have to make it work, to see how they interpret its practicality. Many organizations get stuck because they don't explore the practical obstacles to execution until after the new budget year begins. Only then might the sales department turn to marketing and request a new ad campaign to hit their 10% revenue improvement goal, or turn to engineering to develop an appealing new product. Neither marketing nor engineering had built those requests into their annual plans, because there was no prior alignment on what "increase sales by 10%" would look like in practice.

So the key is to apply the Collective Genius Process regarding what the strategies are and how they will be achieved *before locking in your financial targets*. Then and only then can departments have discussions about what they will need to do differently to support each initiative and budget for it appropriately.

You've probably heard of the acronym SMART (Specific, Meaningful, Actionable, Realistic, Time Bound) to use as criteria for strategic goals. It's an often-used tool, but from my experience in helping leaders design strategic plans, it's missing three critical elements to add the context or background that led to those goals. To help each objective stand on its own, answer these additional questions:

- What is the **activity** to accomplish the objective?
- What is the **measure of completion**?
- What's the **purpose** of accomplishing this goal?

Let's break down these extra elements of activity, measure, and purpose (AMP).

The activity question forces you to address *how* you're going to execute this strategy. Using the example above, the strategy about increasing sales might expand to: "We will increase sales revenue by 10% by selecting two products, redesigning them, and making one of them available on retail shelves with new packaging at a lower price point." There will be a lot of work required to accomplish this goal, but this formulation provides clear direction about what needs to be done. The single owner of this goal will be accountable for making sure it happens. Using this *how* formula for activity, people can spend less time debating their interpretations of the objective and more time executing it.

The clearly defined measure of completion enables an objective third party to identify if a goal has been achieved. Think of measure here as what we will see or experience to let us know the objective was completed. Trapdoor words like *complete* or *introduce* or *develop* are open to interpretation. The important idea is to avoid ambiguity in describing the evidence. Specifics, such as "Every member of customer service will participate in at least one training" or "Marketing will deliver research results in a presentation to the sales executive team," are much more effective.

Finally, identify *why* this goal is important to complete, which you can think of as its purpose. Too often we see managers establish an objective or goal that does not include a mention of why it's important. Purpose usually refers to a customer promise, values, longer-term objectives, or the overarching company's compelling purpose, which will be better achieved when this objective is completed.

Take It for a Road Test

Now that the planning team is satisfied that the wording of a few prioritized new strategies meets the essential criteria, it's time to try them out on a wider audience. Consider which departments will be most involved in successful execution of each strategy. Distribute the summary statement to two or three members of those departments and ask, "What does this mean to you? What would you expect to do as a result?" Each strategic statement should come with no additional explanation, since if it was drafted correctly it will stand on its own.

Listen to the feedback you get from this sample audience. Are people interpreting the strategies consistently, and in line with what the planning team intended? Is there any confusion about what's expected from them? Use the feedback on each strategy to make adjustments as necessary. Don't move forward until you're satisfied that the language is both easy to understand and practical for all involved to implement.

Activate the Plan

At this point in the process, the executive team has worked hard to create a handful of high priority strategies that have the potential to deliver significant improvement for the whole company. They've shared them with key colleagues and the board, if applicable. They've refined the language to make them both clear and practical. And now it's finally approved. Victory!

Not so fast. If the strategy isn't rolled out properly to the full company, all that hard work might end up being a waste of time.

A typical company might email the strategic plan to the full company, with a summary and a big thank-you to all who helped create it. But then . . . nothing really changes. Everyone goes back to their jobs and keeps getting stuff done the way they always have. There might be some lip service toward the new strategy, but before long even that evaporates.

The way to avoid this depressing scenario is to treat activating the strategic plan as just as important as developing the plan. Think hard about what it will take to fully engage all team members and win their buy-in so they will willingly integrate it into their day-to-day activities. This begins by going back to our core principle of "done with, not done to." You don't want the plan to appear to be handed down by an omnipotent authority, like Moses bringing the tablets down from the mountaintop. Activating the plan is all about sharing it not as a done deal, but as a work in progress whose success will depend on everyone's contributions.

We suggest that instead of a company-wide email, department leaders should each circulate the strategies privately to their teams and ask a few key questions:

- What details do we want to clarify about what this plan means to us?
- What are we able to do (if anything) to support each strategy?
- What other departments will we need to coordinate with to make it successful?
- What measures would let us know if we are on track with each strategy?

Then the department leaders can convene a meeting to explore answers to those questions and create subgoals and tactics just for their department to support the overall plan. Some strategies may not apply to certain departments at all. However, as we noted above, all game-changing strategies involve multiple departments, so everyone in the company will likely be affected by at least one aspect of the new plan.

Then a second meeting should be held to review the work of the first session with fresh eyes and possibly revise the department's response, including quarterly milestones and owners assigned for key tactics. Everyone should be alerted that, going forward, progress will be reviewed each week at departmental meetings. At the end of each quarter they can take a deeper look at how well the strategy has been executed and how close the department is to achieving its targets.

The key to this kind of activation is that buy-in is achieved at the departmental level, where people have the most direct contact with their colleagues and immediate leader. The new strategy is not an abstraction sent via email from the CEO; it's immediately a part of everyone's day-to-day practices.

Learn from the Results

The final key step in strategic planning and implementation is setting up a learning loop to improve your next round of the process.

Healthy teams often see the end of a quarter or a year as a time to convene to learn from what happened versus what they expected. This is not the "variance analysis" often requested by a CFO to explain the variance between budgeted and actual metrics. This is about building predictive muscle—taking a qualitative as well as quantitative look at what went well, what went poorly, and why. It's as valuable as an NFL team watching video of their previous game to figure out why their quarterback got sacked so often and why the other team scored four touchdowns.

We can apply Collective Genius to this learning loop, just as we did to the drafting of the original strategy. Start by asking each participant in the strategic review process to ponder these three questions in advance:

- What did we learn about the *scope* of the strategy? Was it too ambitious or not ambitious enough?
- What did we learn about the *wording* of the strategy? Was it clear in describing what we wanted to achieve and how we'd get there?
- What can we learn from the *execution* of the strategy? Did we keep it front and center during the full quarter or year? If certain parts fell by the wayside, why?

Open and honest answers to these questions will allow the team to establish more accurate goals for the upcoming time period and tweak the process to make sure it is even more effective next time.

This review may seem like "just another meeting"—but I promise that it's one of the most important meetings you'll hold all year. By asking people to collaborate to evaluate the impact of the strategy, you once again share collective responsibility with all department heads, and by extension with all of their people. They will have a much stronger incentive to think of each new strategic plan as their own, not one sent down from on high. That will lead to even more buy-in during the next round of goals.

This opportunity to create a learning loop is often overlooked, perhaps because people don't see any value in looking backward rather than forward. Yet it can help an entire organization draw powerful lessons about its capabilities and challenges. As with an NFL team, the point isn't to yell at the offensive line for allowing those quarterback sacks—it's to help them do better next time.

You can keep the planning process alive by repeating these four steps each quarter to "chunk out" the annual plan, apply what you've learned so far, and identify new opportunities. But the plan itself shouldn't change during the year; that would defeat the annual learning cycle and confuse the organization. However, creating quarterly goals to support the annual plan keeps it alive and enables milestones to be celebrated.

By combining the power of these four steps—Map, Test, Activate, Learn— you can transform strategic planning from a routine, boring exercise into a truly transformative experience for your organization and all of its people.

Ideas Worth Considering

1. What is currently working for you in implementing your strategic plans? What isn't?
2. What can you do in your organization to better engage every person in creating and implementing the annual strategic plan?
3. What metrics do you think will be most important to track as you begin to craft new strategies?

CONCLUSION

One day I got a call from the second-generation co-owner of a business
that was struggling. Let me rephrase that, since there was nothing wrong
with the fundamentals of this business. The actual problem was this man's
shattered relationship with his brother, the other co-owner.

I'll never forget sitting in an airport Delta Club, awaiting my flight,
while my new client described years of acrimony and fighting that had followed their dad's passing. While they had worked together well when their
dad was there to resolve disagreements between them, they couldn't figure
out how to get along without him. Now they were both at their wits' end,
and the bad vibes had infected the entire staff. No one felt any engagement
or satisfaction at their jobs. Turnover was rising and profits were declining.
It looked like the only solution would be to sell the business, split the pro-
ceeds, and go their separate ways.

My response: "Before you do anything drastic, don't give up! Lots of
companies get stuck in this kind of situation, where everything seems poi-
soned and hopeless. But I've seen many of them turn things around by
applying a few fairly simple strategies. Let's ask your brother to give it a try
for a few months. If nothing improves, you can always sell at that point."

To their great credit, the brothers were willing to try many of the techniques you've been reading about in this book. They started to apply Collective Genius with each other and then extended it to their whole team. They

practiced the Drama-Free Problem-Solving System. They started leading more effective meetings, focusing on questions rather than answers, and setting fewer but better priorities. And so on.

Within a few short quarters, things improved. And not just morale—the business results were nothing short of amazing. Revenues and profits were both significantly up, turnover was down, and the vibe of the whole company was more optimistic. People on their team felt more empowered because their opinions were now heard and respected, and because they were being treated as future leaders rather than cogs in someone else's machine.

The brothers still disagreed on a lot of issues, sometimes with great passion. But now they could acknowledge their differences without personal hostility. They could talk things over with the team and agree to pursue whatever decisions made the most sense to the most people. Sometimes one brother got his way, and sometimes the other did. More importantly, they stopped making each other—and the whole staff—want to jump out the window. And when they succeeded, they celebrated as equal contributors, just as they had with their dad in the old days.

Working with people like those brothers—and seeing them achieve more than they ever thought possible—is one of the greatest satisfactions of my life. It's why I never want to stop spreading the message of *The Buy-In Advantage*.

I know that applying everything you've been learning, or even some of it, won't be easy. Every learning opportunity comes with challenges. It's often faster and easier to leap in and solve problems on your own instead of including your people. But unless it's a legitimate emergency, resist that temptation! Think about how to accept some short-term discomfort or frustration today in exchange for developing a team that will drive better results tomorrow.

As I often tell clients, organizational success is a *process*, not an event. It's the result of doing the right things over and over, day after day, in both major and minor situations. That's how you grow people, inspire them with a compelling purpose, create and sustain their buy-in, and enjoy the payoff down the road. The only real alternative is to get stuck on the hamster wheel of repeating crises, one after another, spending your whole career chasing a potentially better future that will probably never arrive.

If you feel stuck on that hamster wheel right now, and perhaps overwhelmed by how much material we covered in this book, don't try to fix everything at once! Pick just one chapter that you think is most relevant to your current situation. Share its ideas with your team and start to implement them—even if you have to take baby steps at first. Getting unstuck isn't a race. Get the hang of one technique, then try a second. If you see progress—which I bet you will—it will motivate you and your team to keep going.

At the end of the day, no matter what field we're in, we're all looking for basically the same things at work. Not merely fair compensation, though of course that's still important. Virtually everyone also seeks recognition for our contributions . . . a sense that our work is meaningful and we can be proud of it . . . a feeling that we like and respect our colleagues and leaders. In short, we all want to feel the Buy-In Advantage!

I hope you will enjoy challenging yourself and your colleagues to make some powerful changes to create that advantage. Have fun applying the techniques we've reviewed here.

I'd love to hear from you about your progress and any other ideas that work for you. You can reach out anytime: engage@garrisongrowth.com.

Onward! And thanks for reading.

–Dave

READY FOR MORE?

If you made it to this point in the book, you're probably thinking about how you can increase buy-in and help your team and organization create game-changing results.

In addition to the strategies we've outlined in the book, here are some additional steps you can take to press "fast forward" on your results.

- Share this book with your leadership team and together identify which best practices can benefit the organization the most. Then have their teams do the same exercise. (Contact us for an introduction to booksellers if you would like bulk discounts.)
- Subscribe to the Garrison Growth newsletter and take advantage of the discussion questions and tool case examples to start conversations with your team.
- Join our fireside chats to learn more about what's working right now in solving timely leadership challenges. Subscribe to the newsletter to get the latest invite.
- Contact us to request our proprietary assessment tools, so we can help you figure out what areas to focus on to get the quickest results.
- Inquire about our interactive workshops for your management team (or all employees!), virtually or in person, to help

you achieve your strategic goals and priorities with the Buy-In Advantage.

- Hire Dave to deliver an engaging, actionable keynote for your annual meeting, conference, or industry association meeting that gives the audience powerful ideas they can start to implement right away.
- Ask about our certification program to train and equip your leaders to align and execute strategy as well as increase buy-in with their teams.
- Reach out if you need a custom solution to help solve your buy-in challenge and achieve your unique goals.
- We can customize our training tools for your unique needs, after we connect with you to figure out what you need on your journey toward the Buy-In Advantage.

For any or all of the above, please contact the Garrison Growth team at engage@garrisongrowth.com or use the QR code below to learn more.

ACKNOWLEDGMENTS

Late one evening about 15 years ago, I was walking up Broadway in New York City after a celebratory dinner. I passed a window that I assumed was a bookstore, but it only had three books on display. Baffled at this poor use of merchandising space, I soon realized that it wasn't a bookstore after all, but the ground floor of a publishing house. I wondered if I'd ever have an opportunity to turn my own ideas and experiences into a book.

Even now, as I put the final touches on *The Buy-In Advantage*, it's hard to believe that I've finally joined the community of authors. Getting to this point has been a true team effort. I can't begin to name and properly thank all those who have inspired and supported me along the way, but I'll try.

First and foremost, my wife, Nancy, is a teacher of entrepreneurs through the Goldman Sachs Foundation's 10,000 Small Businesses program, as well as a loving partner through the ups and downs of my journey—even when we needed to float Garrison Growth on credit cards. Our daughter, Emma, was on the management fast track at Target when she insisted on joining the business instead, and she has since been an outstanding partner. Our son, John, is an officer in the US Air Force and an F-16 instructor pilot who has flown in multiple combat zones; he even invited me to facilitate a session on "Leadership at the Speed of Sound." I am eternally grateful to all three for sharing their experiences, ideas, and support for this book.

The Young Presidents' Organization (YPO), representing more than 30,000 leaders around the globe, has been my home away from home for many years. In particular, serving on the YPO International Networks, Events, and Learning Committees has introduced me to some amazingly successful individuals, some of whom graciously agreed to share their stories in this book. Being invited to facilitate YPO Global Board meetings has taught me huge lessons about managing a diverse, driven group of leaders across a dozen countries. In addition, my YPO forum mates in California, Utah, and Arizona have inspired and challenged me, making this book better. They include Mike Hexner, a lifelong friend who always tells me what he thinks, even when I don't want to hear his invaluable feedback.

This book would not have been possible without the trust and support from Garrison Growth's clients, who have reminded me again and again what works and what doesn't in the real world. The mission that keeps our team going is seeing our clients accomplish things they did not think possible, using our tools coupled with their own experiences and insights. I am especially grateful for those clients who kindly granted me permission to tell their stories in these pages.

You may have also noticed stories about some of my neighbors in Park City, Utah. Longtime friends Jeff Edison and Shari Levitin stimulated my thinking during this book's multi-year journey to publication.

The Garrison Growth team deserves a shout-out as well. Each member wears multiple hats to "create great" in partnership with our clients. The ideas and energy behind our newsletters, workshops, fireside chats, and client interactions are all a team effort. We practice what we preach as best we can.

My classmates from Harvard Business School are another source of inspiration. We gather every quarter to share insights and life lessons that keep my thinking fresh. It's fun to be on this journey through business and life with them.

This book was only possible thanks to an amazing team of editors, advisors, and publishing professionals. While the model and concepts are mine, if you like the writing please join me in thanking my strategic partners, Elizabeth Marshall and Will Weisser. Every step of the way, they have given me excellent feedback on the structure, stories, and language choices. My Garrison Growth colleague Christina Warner has also been an essential contributor to the editorial process.

The BenBella / Matt Holt Books team believed in us and gave us outstanding support to bring this book to market, starting from the moment Editor-in-Chief Matt Holt decided to publish it. Managing Editor Katie Dickman and Associate Editor Lydia Choi have spent many hours providing direction and meaningful feedback. Others on the BenBella team have done an amazing job on the interior design, typesetting, cover design, marketing, and all the other details that make a book possible. My deepest gratitude to them all.

Most of all, thank *you* for supporting our community by investing your time and effort in this book and these ideas. I trust you will put them to good use, improve on them, tell others about them, and share your insights with our community.

NOTES

Part 1

1   Jim Harter, "U.S. Engagement Hits 11-Year Low," April 10, 2024, Gallup, https://www.gallup.com/workplace/643286/engagement-hits-11-year-low.aspx.
2   Eric Reed, "What Is the S&P 500 Average Annual Return?" SmartAsset, April 24, 2024, https://smartasset.com/investing/sp-500-average-annual-return.

Chapter 1

1   Matt Tenney, "The Cost of Low Employee Engagement," Business Leadership Today, accessed August 13, 2024, https://businessleadershiptoday.com/the-cost-of-low-employee-engagement/.
2   "Culture & Cash Connection: New Report Ties Revenue Growth to Companies with Healthy Cultures," Grant Thornton, April 2, 2019, https://www.grantthornton.com/insights/press-releases/2019/april/culture-cash-connection.
3   "High School Completion Rate Is Highest in US History," US Census Bureau, December 14, 2017, https://www.census.gov/newsroom/press-releases/2017/educational-attainment-2017.html; https://www.statista.com/statistics/184260/educational-attainment-in-the-us/.
4   Kevin Carey, "The Myth of the Unemployed College Grad," The Atlantic, December 17, 2023, https://www.theatlantic.com/ideas/archive/2023/12/myth-unemployed-college-grad/676364/.
5   "Quotes," Eisenhower Presidential Library website, accessed August 13, 2024, https://www.eisenhowerlibrary.gov/eisenhowers/quotes.

Chapter 2

1   "Nicholas Bloom predicts a working-from-home Nike swoosh," By Invitation, Economist, August 29, 2023, https://www.economist.com/by-invitation/2023/08/29/

nicholas-bloom-predicts-a-working-from-home-nike-swoosh.

2   Naina Dhingra, Andrew Samo, Bill Schaninger, and Matt Schrimper, "Help Your Employees Find Purpose—Or Watch Them Leave," McKinsey & Company, April 5, 2021, https://www.mckinsey.com/capabilities/people-and-organizational-performance/our-insights/help-your-employees-find-purpose-or-watch-them-leave.

3   Alok Patel and Stephanie Plowman, "The Increasing Importance of a Best Friend at Work," Gallup, August 17, 2022, https://www.gallup.com/workplace/397058/increasing-importance-best-friend-work.aspx.

4   Vipula Gandhi and Jennifer Robison, "The 'Great Resignation' Is Really the 'Great Discontent,'" Gallup, July 22, 2021, https://www.gallup.com/workplace/351545/great-resignation-really-great-discontent.aspx.

5   "The Real Cost of Employee Turnover (And How to Prevent It)," Jobvite, February 19, 2024, https://www.jobvite.com/blog/cost-of-employee-turnover/.

6   "The Benefits of Employee Engagement," Gallup, January 7, 2023, https://www.gallup.com/workplace/236927/employee-engagement-drives-growth.aspx.

7   *Firms of Endearment* website, accessed August 13, 2024, https://firmsofendearment.com/.

8   "What Is the S&P 500 Average Annual Return?", accessed September 5, 2024, https://smartasset.com/investing/sp-500-average-annual-return.

9   Will Guidara, *Unreasonable Hospitality: The Remarkable Power of Giving People More Than They Expect* (New York: Optimism Press, 2022).

10   Nitin Nohria, Boris Groysberg, and Linda-Eling Lee, "Employee Motivation: A Powerful New Model," *Harvard Business Review*, July–August 2008, https://hbr.org/2008/07/employee-motivation-a-powerful-new-model.

Chapter 3

1   Heidi Tolliver-Walker, "Want to Improve Productivity? Increase Employee Engagement," *WhatTheyThink*, July 12, 2023, https://whattheythink.com/articles/115757-want-improve-productivity-increase-employee-engagement/.

2   Alison Beard and Steven Rogelberg, "Why Meetings Go Wrong (And How to Fix Them)," November 5, 2019, in *HBR IdeaCast*, produced by *Harvard Business Review*, podcast, 29:04, https://hbr.org/podcast/2019/11/why-meetings-go-wrong-and-how-to-fix-them.

3   Jim Harter, "In New Workplace, US Employee Engagement Stagnates," Gallup, January 23, 2024, https://www.gallup.com/workplace/608675/new-workplace-employee-engagement-stagnates.aspx.

Chapter 4

1   The process we've developed is based in part on the Liberating Structures work of Keith McCandless. You can learn more about his work at liberatingstructures.com.

2   Natasha Tamiru, "Team Dynamics: Five Keys to Building Effective Teams," Think with Google, June 2023, https://www.thinkwithgoogle.com/intl/en-emea/consumer-insights/consumer-trends/five-dynamics-effective-team/.

3   Paul J. Zak, "The Neuroscience of Trust," *Harvard Business Review*, January–February

2017, https://hbr.org/2017/01/the-neuroscience-of-trust.

4   "The Disney Creative Strategy," MindTools, accessed August 13, 2024, https://www.mindtools.com/abyeaeb/the-disney-creative-strategy.

5   Shari Levitin, interview with the author, 2022.

6   Suzie Gruber, "Explore—Curiosity as a Bridge to Aliveness," LinkedIn (blog), March 30, 2016, https://www.linkedin.com/pulse/explore-curiosity-bridge-aliveness-suzie-gruber/.

7   James Surowiecki, *The Wisdom of Crowds* (New York: Knopf Doubleday Publishing Group, 2005).

8   You can also find some case studies on our website: garrisongrowth.com/collectivegenius.

9   Beau Johnson, interview with the author, 2021.

Chapter 5

1   Daniel Kahneman, *Thinking, Fast and Slow* (New York: Farrar, Straus and Giroux, 2011).

2   Colin Powell, *My American Journey* (New York: Random House, 1995).

3   Justin Fox, "Don't Play with Dead Snakes, and Other Management Advice," *Harvard Business Review*, June 25, 2014, https://hbr.org/2014/06/dont-play-with-dead-snakes-and-other-management-advice.

Chapter 6

1   "Will GE Do Better as Three Companies Than as One?" *Economist*, April 2, 2024, https://www.economist.com/business/2024/04/02/will-ge-do-better-as-three-companies-than-as-one.

Chapter 7

1   "2022 Microsoft Work Trend Index Special Report," Microsoft, September 22, 2022, https://www.microsoft.com/en-us/worklab/work-trend-index/hybrid-work-is-just-work.

2   Goodreads, David Packard quote, https://www.goodreads.com/quotes/7183766-he-said-that-more-businesses-die-from-indigestion-than-starvation.

3   "Starbucks Ends the Fiscal 2015 with Stronger Comparable Store Sales," *Forbes*, November 2, 2015, https://www.forbes.com/sites/greatspeculations/2015/11/02/starbucks-ends-the-fiscal-2015-with-stronger-comparable-store-sales/.

4   Taylor Soper, "Starbucks Mobile Orders Surpass 30% of Total Transactions at US Stores," GeekWire, January 31, 2024, https://www.geekwire.com/2024/starbucks-mobile-orders-surpass-30-of-total-transactions-at-u-s-stores-for-the-first-time/.

Chapter 8

1   Carl Von Wodtke and Aviation History Magazine, "This Is the Story of Heather 'Lucky' Penney, Who Was Asked to Do the Unthinkable on 9/11," Military Times, September 11, 2016, https://www.militarytimes.com/2016/09/11/this-is-the-story-of-heather-lucky-penney-who-was-asked-to-do-the-unthinkable-on-9-11/.

2   John P. Kotter, "What Leaders Really Do," *Harvard Business Review*, December 2001, https://hbr.org/2001/12/what-leaders-really-do.

3   Ibid.

4   Ryan Niles, interview with the author, 2019.

Chapter 9

1   This is one example of a feelings wheel, based on the following: G. Willcox, "The Feeling Wheel: A Tool for Expanding Awareness of Emotions and Increasing Spontaneity and Intimacy," *Transactional Analysis Journal* 12(4) (1982): 274–76, https://doi.org/10.1177/036215378201200411.

Chapter 10

1   "Walmart Slogan: 'Save Money. Live Better.' Meaning," 8th & Walton, May 31, 2022, https://www.8thandwalton.com/blog/walmart-slogan/.

2   Simon Sinek, *Start with Why: How Great Leaders Inspire Everyone to Take Action* (London: Penguin Books, 2011).

3   Daniel Goleman, "Millennials: The Purpose Generation," Korn Ferry, accessed August 14, 2024, https://www.kornferry.com/insights/this-week-in-leadership/millennials-purpose-generation.

4   Daniel Goleman, "Don't Think Purpose Is Important? Gen Zers Do," Korn Ferry, accessed August 14, 2024, https://www.kornferry.com/insights/this-week-in-leadership/dont-think-purpose-is-important-gen-zers-do.

5   Phil Kirschner, Adrian Kwok, Matt Schrimper, and Brook Weddle, "Your Office Needs a Purpose," McKinsey & Company, August 29, 2022, https://www.mckinsey.com/capabilities/people-and-organizational-performance/our-insights/the-organization-blog/your-office-needs-a-purpose.

6   Bruce Jones, "How Disney Encourages Employees to Deliver Exceptional Customer Service," *Harvard Business Review*, February 28, 2018, https://hbr.org/sponsored/2018/02/how-disney-encourages-employees-to-deliver-exceptional-customer-service.

7   "What Is Nike's Mission?" Nike website, accessed August 14, 2024, https://www.nike.com/help/a/nikeinc-mission.

8   "Careers," Morgan Jewelers website, accessed August 29, 2024, https://www.morganjewelers.com/careers.

9   This purpose was offered directly to the author from the copresidents of the company. You can also find this phrase on their website, here: "Who We Are," Aero-Graphics website, accessed August 29, 2024, https://www.aero-graphics.com/about-aero-graphics/.

10   "Purpose, Values, and Culture," Campbell's website, accessed August 29, 2024, https://www.campbellsoupcompany.com/about-us/purpose-values-culture/.

11   "Mission, Values & History," Food Gatherers website, accessed August 14, 2024, https://www.foodgatherers.org/about-us/mission-values-history/.

Chapter 11

1   "The Key to Financially Recovering from COVID-19: Engaging Your Employees," CHG Healthcare, May 18, 2020, https://chghealthcare.com/blog/the-key-to-financially-recovering-from-covid-19-engaging-your-employees.

Chapter 12

1   "Passenger Is Charged in Disruption of Flight," *New York Times*, August 7, 1988, https://www.nytimes.com/1988/08/07/us/passenger-is-charged-in-disruption-of-flight.html.

2   "From Praise to Profits: The Business Case for Recognition at Work," Gallup, accessed August 14, 2024, https://assets.ctfassets.net/hff6luki1ys4/2gLQxQeHWTXD4cNXneh3u5/6c97825b0fd14768573c44af39add741/from-praise-to-profits-the-business-case-for-recognition-at-work__2_.pdf.

3   Dhingra, Samo, Schaninger, and Schrimper, "Help Your Employees Find Purpose."

4   Aditi Shrikant, "63% of Gen Z Workers Have a Best Friend in the Office—There Are 2 Potential Drawbacks, Experts Say," CNBC, November 14, 2023, https://www.cnbc.com/2023/11/14/glassdoor-survey-63percent-of-gen-z-workers-have-a-best-friend-at-work.html.

5   Allen Glines, "Dutch Bros Apparel: A Hidden Gem Not for Public Sale," Medium, November 21, 2023, https://imallenglines.medium.com/dutch-bros-apparel-a-hidden-gem-not-for-public-sale-01039962e7cf.

6   Starbucks Careers page, Starbucks website, https://www.starbucks.com/careers/.

7   Careers tab, Dutch Bros Coffee website, accessed August 14, 2024, https://www.dutchbros.com/employment.

8   Johnathan Maze, "Dutch Bros Speeds Development, Thanks to Its Low Turnover," Restaurant Business Online, March 2, 2022, https://www.restaurantbusinessonline.com/financing/dutch-bros-speeds-development-thanks-its-low-turnover; Starbucks 2023 Global Impact Report. https://stories.starbucks.com/uploads/2024/02/2023-Starbucks-Global-Impact-Report-Partner-Data-Tables.pdf.

9   Rachel Rabkin Peachman, "America's Best Large Employers," *Forbes*, February 13, 2024, https://www.forbes.com/lists/best-large-employers/?sh=5e8a2d2a7b66.

10   Raising Cane's Careers website, accessed August 14, 2024, https://jobs.raisingcanes.com/.

11   Careers tab, KFC website, accessed August 14, 2024, https://www.kfc.com/careers.

12   Culture tab, Target Corporate website, accessed August 14, 2024, https://corporate.target.com/careers/culture.

Chapter 13

1   Ann Schmidt, "How Fred Smith Rescued FedEx from Bankruptcy by Playing Blackjack in Las Vegas," Fox Business, July 19, 2020, https://www.foxbusiness.com/money/fred-smith-fedex-blackjack-winning-formula.

2   Patrick Lencioni, *The 6 Types of Working Genius: A Better Way to Understand Your Gifts, Your Frustrations, and Your Team* (Dallas: Matt Holt Books, 2022).

3   Lena Gerber, "DaVita CEO Kent Thiry's Leadership: From Bankruptcy to a

Healthcare Leadership Model," CU Denver Business School Newsroom, University of Colorado Denver website, May 3, 2018, https://business-news.ucdenver. edu/2018/05/03/conversation-healthcare-ceo-fortune-500-company/.

4   Patrick Lencioni, *The Five Dysfunctions of a Team: A Leadership Fable* (San Francisco: Jossey-Bass, 2002).

5   Chuck Ulie, "Maverick CEO Chuck Maggelet Retiring, Crystal Maggelet Taking Over in Interim," CSP Daily News, March 8, 2024, https://www.cspdailynews.com/ company-news/maverik-ceo-chuck-maggelet-retiring-crystal-maggelet-taking-over- interim.

Chapter 14

1   You can find a reader's bonus on how to do this on our website: garrisongrowth.com /bookresources.

ABOUT THE AUTHOR

Photo by Matt Davies Photography

Dave Garrison is a recognized expert in developing the business and people strategy that's needed to create game-changing results. He has more than 25 years of experience as a CEO, strategic advisor, and independent board member for public and private companies, such as Ameritrade, both in the United States and internationally.

He cofounded Garrison Growth in 2013 to help organizations, ranging from new startups to major public corporations, get the best possible results from their teams. Thousands of leaders who have taken the firm's practices to heart have enjoyed dramatic improvements in profitability, retention, and team buy-in and significant results from applying their Strategic Alignment and Accountability System (SAAS), the Collective Genius Process, and other proprietary frameworks.

Dave has been an active member of the Young Presidents' Organization (YPO) since 1993. He has conducted workshops with thousands of YPO leaders and has been selected by his peers to serve on select global YPO committees including Events, Networks, and Learning. Currently, he is the chair of the YPO's Leadership Development Network, which has nearly 10,000 qualified CEOs as members.

He is a sought-after keynote speaker, workshop facilitator, executive coach, and leadership expert for media outlets such as CNBC, CNN, and the *Wall Street Journal*. A lifelong learner, Dave has an MBA from Harvard Business School and has been trained in the Entrepreneurial Operating System (EOS), neuro-linguistic programming, and DISC.

When he's not working with clients, Dave is an avid sailor, golfer, pilot, and traveler. He and his family live in Oro Valley, Arizona, and Park City, Utah.